studysync®

Reading & Writing Companion

Our Heroes

studysync

studysync.com

11 LWI 21   B

STUDENT GUIDE

GETTING STARTED

Welcome to the StudySync Reading and Writing Companion! In this booklet, you will find a collection of readings based on the theme of the unit you are studying. As you work through the readings, you will be asked to answer questions and perform a variety of tasks designed to help you closely analyze and understand each text selection. Read on for an explanation of

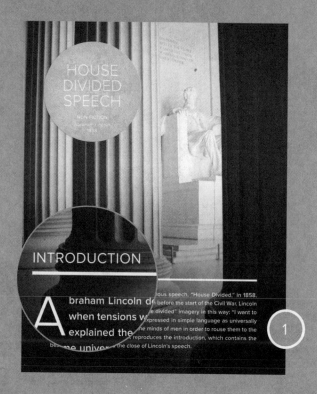

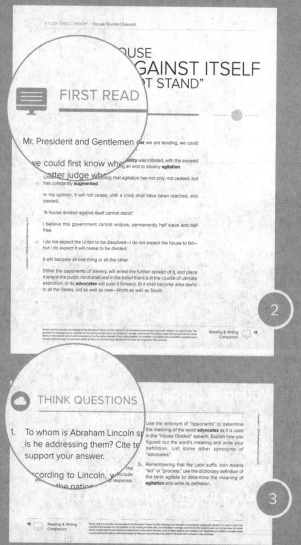

1 INTRODUCTION

An Introduction to each text provides historical context for your reading as well as information about the author. You will also learn about the genre of the excerpt and the year in which it was written.

2 FIRST READ

During your first reading of each excerpt, you should just try to get a general idea of the content and message of the reading. Don't worry if there are parts you don't understand or words that are unfamiliar to you. You'll have an opportunity later to dive deeper into the text.

Many times, while working through the Think Questions after your first read, you will be asked to **annotate** or **make annotations** about what you are reading. This means that you should use the "Notes" column to make comments or jot down any questions you may have about the text. You may also want to note any unfamiliar vocabulary words here.

3 THINK QUESTIONS

These questions will ask you to start thinking critically about the text, asking specific questions about its purpose, and making connections to your prior knowledge and reading experiences. To answer these questions, you should go back to the text and draw upon specific evidence that you find there to support your responses. You will also begin to explore some of the more challenging vocabulary words used in the excerpt.

CLOSE READ & FOCUS QUESTIONS

After you have completed the First Read, you will then be asked to go back and read the excerpt more closely and critically. Before you begin your Close Read, you should read through the Focus Questions to get an idea of the concepts you will want to focus on during your second reading. You should work through the Focus Questions by making annotations, highlighting important concepts, and writing notes or questions in the "Notes" column. Depending on instructions from your teacher, you may need to respond online or use a separate piece of paper to start expanding on your thoughts and ideas.

WRITING PROMPT

Your study of each excerpt or selection will end with a writing assignment. To complete this assignment, you should use your notes, annotations, and answers to both the Think and Focus Questions. Be sure to read the prompt carefully and address each part of it in your writing assignment.

EXTENDED WRITING PROJECT

After you have read and worked through all of the unit text selections, you will move on to a writing project. This project will walk you through steps to plan, draft, revise, edit, and finally publish an essay or other piece of writing about one or more of the texts you have studied in the unit. Student models and graphic organizers will provide guidance and help you organize your thoughts as you plan and write your essay. Throughout the project, you will also study and work on specific writing skills to help you develop different portions of your writing.

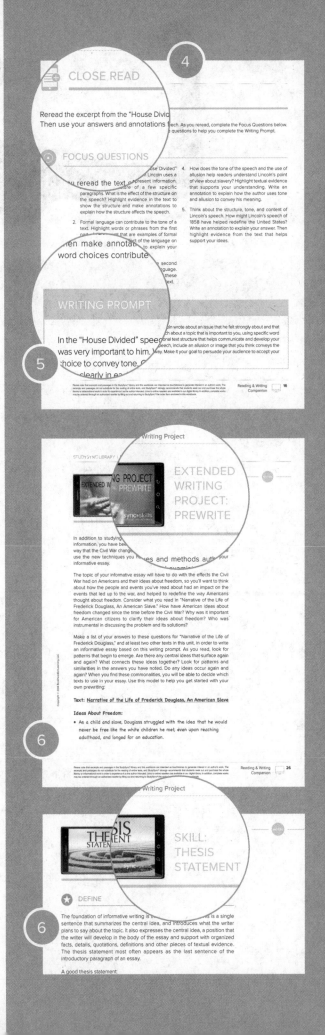

UNIT 4   What does it mean to be a hero?

Our Heroes

TEXTS

TEXTS

EXTENDED WRITING PROJECT

113

Text Fulfillment through StudySync

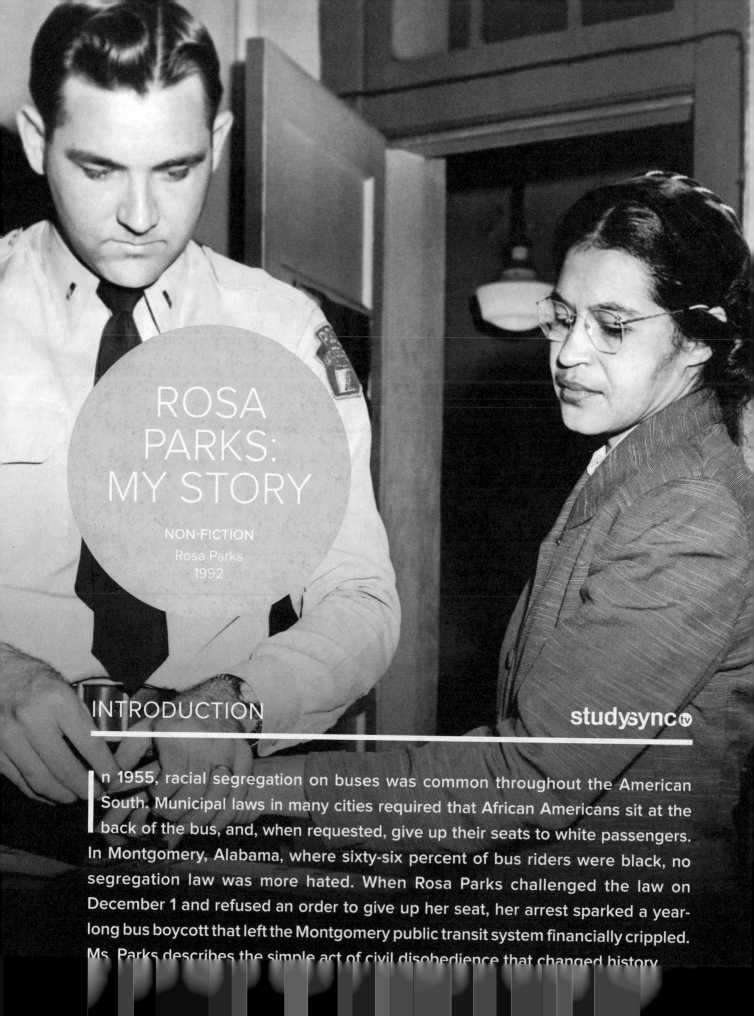

ROSA PARKS: MY STORY

NON-FICTION
Rosa Parks
1992

INTRODUCTION

n 1955, racial segregation on buses was common throughout the American South. Municipal laws in many cities required that African Americans sit at the back of the bus, and, when requested, give up their seats to white passengers. In Montgomery, Alabama, where sixty-six percent of bus riders were black, no segregation law was more hated. When Rosa Parks challenged the law on December 1 and refused an order to give up her seat, her arrest sparked a year-long bus boycott that left the Montgomery public transit system financially crippled. Ms. Parks describes the simple act of civil disobedience that changed history.

studysync tv

"I saw a vacant seat in the middle section of the bus and took it."

 FIRST READ

 NOTES

Excerpt from Chapter 8: "You're Under Arrest"

1 When I got off from work that evening of December 1, I went to Court Square as usual to catch the Cleveland Avenue bus home. I didn't look to see who was driving when I got on, and by the time I recognized him, I had already paid my fare. It was the same driver who had put me off the bus back in 1943, twelve years earlier. He was still tall and heavy, with red, rough-looking skin. And he was still mean-looking. I didn't know if he had been on that route before—they switched the drivers around sometimes. I do know that most of the time if I saw him on a bus, I wouldn't get on it.

2 I saw a vacant seat in the middle section of the bus and took it. I didn't even question why there was a vacant seat even though there were quite a few people standing in the back. If I had thought about it at all, I would probably have figured maybe someone saw me get on and did not take the seat but left it vacant for me. There was a man sitting next to the window and two women across the aisle.

3 The next stop was the Empire Theater, and some whites got on. They filled up the white seats, and one man was left standing. The driver looked back and noticed the man standing. Then he looked back at us. He said, "Let me have those front seats," because they were the front seats of the black section. Didn't anybody move. We just sat right where we were, the four of us. Then he spoke a second time: "Y'all better make it light on yourselves and let me have those seats."

4 The man in the window seat next to me stood up, and I moved to let him pass by me, and then I looked across the aisle and saw that the two women were also standing. I moved over to the window seat. I could not see how standing up was going to "make it light" for me. The more we gave in and **complied**, the worse they treated us.

5   I thought back to the time when I used to sit up all night and didn't sleep, and my grandfather would have his gun right by the fireplace, or if he had his one-horse wagon going anywhere, he always had his gun in the back of the wagon. People always say that I didn't give up my seat because I was tired, but that isn't true. I was not tired physically, or no more tired than I usually was at the end of a working day. I was not old, although some people have an image of me as being old then. I was forty-two. No, the only tired I was, was tired of giving in.

6   The driver of the bus saw me still sitting there, and he asked was I going to stand up. I said, "No." He said, "Well, I'm going to have you arrested." Then I said, "You may do that." These were the only words we said to each other. I didn't even know his name, which was James Blake, until we were in court together. He got out of the bus and stayed outside for a few minutes, waiting for the police.

7   As I sat there, I tried not to think about what might happen. I knew that anything was possible. I could be **manhandled** or beaten. I could be arrested. People have asked me if it occurred to me then that I could be the test case the NAACP had been looking for. I did not think about that at all. In fact if I had let myself think too deeply about what might happen to me, I might have gotten off the bus. But I chose to remain.

8   Meanwhile there were people getting off the bus and asking for transfers, so that began to loosen up the crowd, especially in the back of the bus. Not everyone got off, but everybody was very quiet. What conversation there was, was in low tones; no one was talking out loud. It would have been quite interesting to have seen the whole bus empty out. Or if the other three had stayed where they were, because if they'd had to arrest four of us instead of one, then that would have given me a little support. But it didn't matter. I never thought hard of them at all and never even bothered to criticize them.

9   Eventually two policemen came. They got on the bus, and one of them asked me why I didn't stand up. I asked him, "Why do you all push us around?" He said to me, and I quote him exactly, "I don't know, but the law is the law and you're under arrest." One policeman picked up my purse, and the second one picked up my shopping bag and escorted me to the squad car. In the squad car they returned my personal belongings to me. They did not put their hands on me or force me into the car. After I was seated in the car, they went back to the driver and asked him if he wanted to swear out a **warrant**. He answered that he would finish his route and then come straight back to swear out the warrant. I was only in **custody**, not legally arrested, until the warrant was signed.

10 As they were driving me to the city desk, at City Hall, near Court Street, one of them asked me again, "Why didn't you stand up when the driver spoke to you?" I did not answer. I remained silent all the way to City Hall.

11 As we entered the building, I asked if I could have a drink of water, because my throat was real dry. There was a fountain, and I was standing right next to it. One of the policemen said yes, but by the time I bent down to drink, another policeman said, "No, you can't drink no water. You have to wait until you get to the jail." So I was denied the chance to drink a sip of water. I was not going to do anything but wet my throat. I wasn't going to drink a whole lot of water, even though I was quite thirsty. That made me angry, but I did not respond.

12 At the city desk they filled out the necessary forms as I answered questions such as what my name was and where I lived. I asked if I could make a telephone call and they said, "No." Since that was my first arrest, I didn't know if that was more **discrimination** because I was black or if it was standard practice. But it seemed to me to be more discrimination. Then they escorted me back to the squad car, and we went to the city jail on North Ripley Street.

13 I wasn't frightened at the jail. I was more resigned than anything else. I don't recall being real angry, not enough to have an argument. I was just prepared to accept whatever I had to face. I asked again if I could make a telephone call. I was ignored.

14 They told me to put my purse on the counter and to empty my pockets of personal items. The only thing I had in my pocket was a tissue. I took that out. They didn't search me or handcuff me.

15 I was then taken to an area where I was fingerprinted and where mug shots were taken. A white matron came to escort me to my jail cell, and I asked again if I might use the telephone. She told me that she would find out.

16 She took me up a flight of stairs (the cells were on the second level), through a door covered with iron mesh, and along a dimly lighted corridor. She placed me in an empty dark cell and slammed the door closed. She walked a few steps away, but then she turned around and came back. She said, "There are two girls around the other side, and if you want to go over there with them instead of being in a cell by yourself, I will take you over there."

Excerpted from Rosa Parks: My Story by Rosa Parks, published by Puffin Books.

THINK QUESTIONS

1. Refer to one or more details in the text to explain how Rosa's previous interaction with the bus driver may have contributed to her actions on December 1—both from ideas that are directly stated and ideas that you have inferred from evidence in the text.

2. Use details from the text to explain other factors Parks believes contributed to her actions on December 1, 1955. What do other people seem to think contributed, and does Parks agree?

3. Based on the historical context, how do the law enforcement officials behave in expected and unexpected ways during Rosa's arrest? What inferences can you make from this behavior? Support your answer with textual evidence.

4. Use context to determine the meaning of the word **complied** as it is used in *Rosa: Parks: My Story*. Write your definition of *complied* and tell how you got it.

5. The Latin word *discriminare*, from which *discrimination* comes, means "to separate." Use this knowledge along with the context clues provided in the passage to determine the meaning of **discrimination**. Write your definition of *discrimination* and tell how you got it.

CLOSE READ

Reread the excerpt from *Rosa Parks: My Story*. As you reread, complete the Focus Questions below. Then use your answers and annotations from the questions to help you complete the Writing Prompt.

FOCUS QUESTIONS

1. Based on paragraphs 1 and 2, analyze how Rosa Parks introduced herself. What additional information do you learn about Parks' character from the details she shares? Highlight evidence from the text and make annotations to explain your analysis.

2. In paragraph 5, Parks used the word *tired* repeatedly. Why does she repeat the word? What effect does this create? Discuss the denotations and connotations of this word as Parks used it. Highlight textual evidence and make annotations to explain your response.

3. In paragraph 13, Parks said that she was not frightened or angry but "resigned" to the consequences of the situation. Which details in previous paragraphs illustrate this attitude? Support your answer with textual evidence and make annotations to explain your response.

4. In paragraph 16, explain how Parks used word denotation and connotation to create the mood of the jail. Highlight evidence from the text and make annotations to support your explanation.

5. Based on the text, is Rosa Parks a hero? Why or why not? Highlight textual evidence and make annotations to explain your evaluation.

WRITING PROMPT

The excerpt you read from *Rosa Parks: My Story* is part of Parks's autobiography, a non-fiction narrative she wrote to tell about her life. In it, she introduces and elaborates on a time when she behaved in a very courageous way. Using the excerpt as a model, write a real-life story, or personal narrative, about a time when you responded to a conflict or problem in a brave, kind, or generous way. What was the problem or conflict? Was anyone else involved in the experience or situation? How was the problem or conflict resolved? Remember that your personal narrative should be told from the first-person point of view. Introduce and elaborate on your experience with details and examples, and use transitions to help readers follow the sequence of events. Include description, dialogue, and precise or sensory language to capture and hold readers' attention. Try to use words with connotations that support the overall mood and tone of your narrative. Finally, consider what you learned from your experience. What theme or message might you want to share with your readers in your personal narrative?

Please note that excerpts and passages in the StudySync® library and this workbook are intended as touchstones to generate interest in an author's work. The excerpts and passages do not substitute for the reading of entire texts, and StudySync® strongly recommends that students seek out and purchase the whole literary or informational work in order to experience it as the author intended. Links to online resellers are available in our digital library. In addition, complete works may be ordered through an authorized reseller by filling out and returning to StudySync® the order form enclosed in this workbook.

Reading & Writing Companion 9

THE STORY BEHIND THE BUS

NON-FICTION
The Henry Ford®
2002

INTRODUCTION

The Henry Ford® museum houses a large collection of items of historical significance, including John F. Kennedy's presidential limousine, Abraham Lincoln's seat from Ford's Theatre, and the bus on which civil rights activist Rosa Parks took her famous stand against segregation. This excerpt from the museum's website offers background information on Rosa Parks and the circumstances surrounding her December 1955 arrest in Montgomery, Alabama.

"...Rosa Parks initiated a new era in the American quest for freedom and equality."

FIRST READ

1   On December 1, 1955, Rosa Parks, a 42-year-old African American woman who worked as a seamstress, boarded this Montgomery City bus to go home from work. On this bus on that day, Rosa Parks initiated a new era in the American quest for freedom and equality.

2   She sat near the middle of the bus, just behind the 10 seats reserved for whites. Soon all of the seats in the bus were filled. When a white man entered the bus, the driver (following the standard practice of **segregation**) insisted that all four blacks sitting just behind the white section give up their seats so that the man could sit there. Mrs. Parks, who was an active member of the local NAACP, quietly refused to give up her seat.

3   Her action was spontaneous and not premeditated, although her previous civil rights involvement and strong sense of justice were obvious influences. "When I made that decision," she said later, "I knew that I had the strength of my ancestors with me."

4   She was arrested and convicted of violating the laws of segregation, known as "Jim Crow laws." Mrs. Parks appealed her conviction and thus formally challenged the legality of segregation.

5   At the same time, local civil rights activists initiated a boycott of the Montgomery bus system. In cities across the South, segregated bus companies were daily reminders of the **inequities** of American society. Since African Americans made up about 75 percent of the riders in Montgomery, the boycott posed a serious economic threat to the company and a social threat to white rule in the city.

6   A group named the Montgomery Improvement Association, composed of local activists and ministers, organized the boycott. As their leader, they chose a young Baptist minister who was new to Montgomery: Martin Luther

King, Jr. Sparked by Mrs. Parks' action, the boycott lasted 381 days, into December 1956 when the U.S. Supreme Court ruled that the segregation law was **unconstitutional** and the Montgomery buses were **integrated.** The Montgomery Bus Boycott was the beginning of a revolutionary era of non-violent mass protests in support of civil rights in the United States.

7   It was not just an accident that the civil rights movement began on a city bus. In a famous 1896 case involving a black man on a train, *Plessy v. Ferguson,* the U.S. Supreme Court enunciated the "separate but equal" rationale for Jim Crow. Of course, facilities and treatment were never equal.

8   Under Jim Crow customs and laws, it was relatively easy to separate the races in every area of life except transportation. Bus and train companies couldn't afford separate cars and so blacks and whites had to occupy the same space.

9   Thus, transportation was one of the most **volatile** arenas for race relations in the South. Mrs. Parks remembers going to elementary school in Pine Level, Alabama, where buses took white kids to the new school but black kids had to walk to their school.

10   "I'd see the bus pass every day," she said. "But to me, that was a way of life; we had no choice but to accept what was the custom. *The bus was among the first ways I realized there was a black world and a white world"* (emphasis added).

11   Montgomery's Jim Crow customs were particularly harsh and gave bus drivers great latitude in making decisions on where people could sit. The law even gave bus drivers the authority to carry guns to enforce their edicts. Mrs. Parks' attorney Fred Gray remembered, "Virtually every African-American person in Montgomery had some negative experience with the buses. But we had no choice. We had to use the buses for transportation."

12   Civil rights advocates had outlawed Jim Crow in interstate train travel, and blacks in several Southern cities attacked the practice of segregated bus systems. There had been a bus boycott in Baton Rouge, Louisiana, in 1953, but black leaders compromised before making real gains. Joann Robinson, a black university professor and activist in Montgomery, had suggested the idea of a bus boycott months before the Parks arrest.

13   Two other women had been arrested on buses in Montgomery before Parks and were considered by black leaders as potential clients for challenging the law. However, both were rejected because black leaders felt they would not gain white support. When she heard that the well-respected Rosa Parks had been arrested, one Montgomery African American woman exclaimed, "They've messed with the wrong one now."

14   In the South, city buses were lightning rods for civil rights activists. It took someone with the courage and character of Rosa Parks to strike with lightning. And it required the commitment of the entire African American community to fan the flames ignited by that lightning into the fires of the civil rights revolution.

 THINK QUESTIONS

1. Refer to one or more details from the text to support your understanding of Rosa Parks's statement, "When I made that decision [not to give up my bus seat], I knew that I had the strength of my ancestors with me." Base your explanation both on ideas that are directly stated and ideas that you infer from clues in the text.

2. Use details from the text to explain why the Montgomery bus boycott was particularly effective.

3. Write several sentences explaining why buses were such an important setting for protesters to use for their stance in favor of civil rights. Support your answer with textual evidence.

4. Use context to determine the meaning of the word **segregation** as it is used in "The Story Behind the Bus." Write your definition of *segregation* and tell how you determined it. Then, use a dictionary to check your definition.

5. Use the context clues provided in the passage to determine the meaning of **inequities.** Write your definition of *inequities* and tell how you determined it. Check your definition in context, by using it in place of *inequities* in the sentence.

Please note that excerpts and passages in the StudySync® library and this workbook are intended as touchstones to generate interest in an author's work. The excerpts and passages do not substitute for the reading of entire texts, and StudySync® strongly recommends that students seek out and purchase the whole literary or informational work in order to experience it as the author intended. Links to online resellers are available in our digital library. In addition, complete works may be ordered through an authorized reseller by filling out and returning to StudySync® the order form enclosed in this workbook.

Reading & Writing Companion   **13**

CLOSE READ

Reread the text "The Story Behind the Bus." As you reread, complete the Focus Questions below. Then use your answers and annotations from the questions to help you complete the Writing Prompt.

FOCUS QUESTIONS

1. Which text—*Rosa Parks: My Story* or "The Story Behind the Bus"—does a better job of introducing readers to the character of Rosa Parks? Which text does a better job of helping readers understand the significance of Rosa Parks's actions? Highlight textual evidence in "The Story Behind the Bus" to illustrate what this text accomplishes that is different from what *Rosa Parks: My Story* accomplishes. Make annotations to explain your evaluations.

2. In paragraph 6 of "The Story Behind the Bus," the writer says that Rosa Parks's actions "sparked" the Montgomery bus boycott that followed. Using evidence from the text as well as inferences based on clues in the text, and Parks's own words in paragraph 5 of *Rosa Parks: My Story,* explain why Rosa Parks's actions helped inspire the Montgomery Improvement Association to take action of its own. Make annotations to explain your analysis.

3. In referring to Rosa Parks, an African American woman is quoted as saying, "They've messed with the wrong one now." What do you think she meant by this comment? Base your answer on textual evidence and inferences drawn from clues in the text. Make annotations to explain your conclusions and inferences.

4. In paragraph 10 of "The Story Behind the Bus," Rosa Parks is quoted as saying, "The bus was among the first ways I realized there was a black world and a white world." How does her experience on the bus reflect the wider experience of African Americans in the segregated South? How does Parks describe a similar type of experience in *Rosa Parks: My Story?* Highlight textual evidence and make annotations in "The Story Behind the Bus" and *Rosa Parks: My Story* to support your conclusions and inferences.

5. In what ways have the achievements of the Civil Rights Movement depended not only on heroes such as Rosa Parks and Martin Luther King, Jr., who have achieved recognition for their contributions, but also on heroes such as the African Americans who boycotted the buses for more than a year, yet whose names may not be known to the public or mentioned in accounts such as "The Story Behind the Bus"? Highlight textual evidence and make annotations to explain your ideas.

WRITING PROMPT

Rosa Parks: My Story and "The Story Behind the Bus" both tell about Rosa Parks's famous refusal to give up her seat on a Montgomery bus. However, each author writes for a different purpose and from a different point of view. How are the two presentations of the same event similar and different? Use your understanding of the content as well as purpose, style, and point of view to compare and contrast the two texts. Introduce your writing with a thesis statement. Support your thesis statement with well-organized evidence from the texts, including facts, details, and quotations. Use precise language to explain information, and include transitions as needed to connect ideas. Remember to maintain a formal style in your writing and to reinforce your thesis statement in your conclusion.

Please note that excerpts and passages in the StudySync® library and this workbook are intended as touchstones to generate interest in an author's work. The excerpts and passages do not substitute for the reading of entire texts, and StudySync® strongly recommends that students seek out and purchase the whole literary or informational work in order to experience it as the author intended. Links to online resellers are available in our digital library. In addition, complete works may be ordered through an authorized reseller by filling out and returning to StudySync® the order form enclosed in this workbook.

Reading & Writing
Companion

15

ROSA

POETRY
Rita Dove
1986

INTRODUCTION

Rita Dove is highly regarded African-American poet and author who won the 1987 Pulitzer Prize for Poetry. Dove's poetic works explore a variety of topics, including historical and political events, and she is known for capturing complex emotions succinctly. Her poem "Rosa" is a tribute to Rosa Parks, the activist who helped end segregation by quietly refusing to leave her seat on the bus.

"Doing nothing was the doing..."

 FIRST READ

NOTES

1 How she sat there,
2 the time right inside a place
3 so wrong it was ready.

4 That **trim** name with
5 its dream of a bench
6 to rest on. Her **sensible** coat.

7 Doing nothing was the doing:
8 the clean flame of her gaze
9 **carved** by a camera flash.

10 How she stood up
11 when they bent down to **retrieve**
12 her purse. That **courtesy**.

"Rosa", from ON THE BUS WITH ROSA PARKS by Rita Dove. Copyright © 1999 by Rita Dove. Used by permission of W. W. Norton & Company, Inc.

Please note that excerpts and passages in the StudySync® library and this workbook are intended as touchstones to generate interest in an author's work. The excerpts and passages do not substitute for the reading of entire texts, and StudySync® strongly recommends that students seek out and purchase the whole literary or informational work in order to experience it as the author intended. Links to online resellers are available in our digital library. In addition, complete works may be ordered through an authorized reseller by filling out and returning to StudySync® the order form enclosed in this workbook.

Reading & Writing
Companion

17

THINK QUESTIONS

1. Refer to one or more details from the poem to explain how the setting described in the first stanza is "right" in its wrongness. Base your answer both on ideas that are directly stated and ideas that you infer from the title.

2. Use details from the third stanza and your inferences to explain the speaker's characterization of Parks's action on the bus.

3. Write two or three sentences explaining what happens in the fourth stanza. What does Parks do, and why? What do the officers do, and why? Support your answer with textual evidence and with inferences you make based on textual clues.

4. The word **trim** is an example of a word with multiple meanings. Use context clues from the poem to determine which meaning is being used in "Rosa." Write your definition of *trim* here and tell how you determined it.

5. Remembering that the Latin suffix *-ible* means "able to be," and given that the base word *sense* means "understanding or logic," use these word parts and the context clues provided in the poem to determine the meaning of **sensible.** Write your definition of *sensible* and tell how you determined it.

CLOSE READ

Reread the poem "Rosa." As you reread, complete the Focus Questions below. Then use your answers and annotations from the questions to help you complete the Writing Prompt.

FOCUS QUESTIONS

1. In lines 2 and 3, the speaker uses the antonyms *right* and *wrong*. Discuss how the multiple meanings of each word enhance this word relationship and the meaning of the poem. Highlight textual evidence and make annotations to support your analysis.

2. In lines 4, 5, and 6, Dove makes use of personification—a figure of speech in which an animal, an object, a force of nature, or an idea is given human characteristics—when she suggests that the "name" has a "dream." Discuss the effect of this, and any other, figurative language on Dove's poem. Support your answer with textual evidence and make annotations to explain your analysis.

3. In lines 6 and 12, Dove employs short sentence fragments. Discuss the effect of these elements of poetic structure on Dove's poem. Highlight textual evidence and make annotations to explain your analysis.

4. In line 8, the speaker describes the "clean flame" of Rosa Parks's gaze. Discuss the connotations of these words as they affect the reader's understanding of the image. What other words in this stanza are related to this description, and how? How do these relationships develop the image? Highlight textual evidence and make annotations to explain your analysis.

5. Do you think that Rita Dove believes that Rosa Parks is a hero? Why or why not? How does the structure of the poem support the author's feelings about Rosa Parks? Highlight textual evidence and make annotations to explain your thinking.

WRITING PROMPT

At first glance, Rita Dove's poem "Rosa" appears simple. However, once readers begin to unpack Dove's compact use of poetic structure and language, they find that looks are deceiving. How does Dove use structure and language to create a portrait of the subject of her poem, Rosa Parks? Use your understanding of poetic structure, denotation and connotation, and word relationships to discuss the relationships among form, language, and meaning. Support your writing with textual evidence.

FREEDOM WALKERS:
THE STORY OF THE MONTGOMERY BUS BOYCOTT

NON-FICTION
Russell Freedman
2006

INTRODUCTION

Rosa Parks's famous refusal to give up her seat on a Montgomery, Alabama bus was part of a planned civil action. Nine months earlier, fifteen-year-old Claudette Colvin spontaneously made the same decision, confronting a Montgomery bus driver who told her to move.

"It was against the law for blacks to sit in the same row as a white person."

 FIRST READ

Excerpt from Chapter Two

CLAUDETTE COLVIN

1   "It's my constitutional right!"

2   Two youngsters from New Jersey—sixteen-year-old Edwina Johnson and her brother Marshall, who was fifteen—arrived in Montgomery to visit relatives during the summer of 1949. No one told them about the city's segregation laws for buses, and one day they boarded a bus and sat down by a white man and boy.

3   The white boy told Marshall to get up from the seat beside him. Marshall refused. Then the bus driver ordered the black teenagers to move, but they continued to sit where they were. Up North, they were accustomed to riding integrated buses and trains. They didn't see now why they should give up their seats.

4   The driver called the police, and Edwina and Marshall were arrested. Held in jail for two days, they were convicted at a court hearing of violating the city's segregation laws. Judge Wiley C. Hill threatened to send them to reform school until they were twenty-one, but relatives managed to get them an attorney. They were fined and sent back to New Jersey.

5   During the next few years, other black riders were arrested and convicted for the same offense—sitting in seats reserved for whites. They paid their fines quietly and continued to ride the public buses. It took a spunky fifteen-year-old high school student to bring matters to a head.

6   Claudette Colvin was an A student at all-black Booker T. Washington High. She must have been paying attention in her **civics** classes, for she insisted on applying the lessons she had learned after boarding a city bus on March 2, 1955.

7   Claudette was on her way home from school that day. She found a seat in the middle of the bus, behind the section reserved for whites. As more riders got on, the bus filled up until there were no empty seats left. The aisle was jammed with passengers standing, mostly blacks and a few whites.

8   The driver stopped the bus and ordered black passengers seated behind the white section to get up and move farther back, making more seats available for whites. Reluctantly, black riders gave up their seats and moved into the crowded aisle as whites took over the vacated seats.

9   Claudette didn't move. She knew she wasn't sitting in the **restricted** white section. She felt that she was far enough back to be **entitled** to her seat. A pregnant black woman was sitting next to her: When the driver insisted that the woman get up and stand in the aisle, a black man in the rear offered her his seat, then quickly left the bus to avoid trouble.

10   Claudette was now occupying a double seat alone. "Hey, get up!" the bus driver ordered. Still she refused to move. None of the white women standing would sit in the empty seat next to Claudette. It was against the law for blacks to sit in the same row as a white person.

11   The driver refused to move the bus. "This can't go on," he said. "I'm going to call the cops." He did, and when the police arrived, he demanded that Claudette be arrested.

12   "No," Claudette replied. "I don't have to get up. I paid my fare, so I don't have to get up." At school, Claudette had been studying the U.S. Constitution and the Bill of Rights, and she had taken those lessons to heart. "It's my constitutional right to sit here just as much as that [white] lady," she told the police. "It's my constitutional right!"

13   Blacks had been arrested before for talking back to white officials. Now it was Claudette's turn. She was crying and madder than ever when the police told her she was under arrest. "You have no right to do this," she protested. She struggled as they knocked her books aside, grabbed her wrists, and dragged her off the bus, and she screamed when they put on the handcuffs.

14   "I didn't know what was happening," she said later. "I was just angry. Like a teenager might be, I was just downright angry. It felt like I was helpless." She remained locked up at the city jail until she was bailed out later that day by the pastor of her church.

15   Under Montgomery's segregation laws, Claudette was in fact entitled to her seat behind the whites-only section. If no seats were available for blacks to move back to as additional white passengers boarded the bus, then they were not required to give up their seats. That was the official **policy**. But in

NOTES

actual practice, whenever a white person needed a seat, the driver would order blacks to get up and move to the back of the bus, even when they had to stand in the aisle.

16 Prosecutors threw the book at Claudette. She was charged not only with violating the segregation laws, but also with assault and **battery** for resisting arrest. "She insisted she was colored and just as good as white," the surprised arresting officer told the judge at the court hearing.

17 Claudette's arrest galvanized the black community. E.D. Nixon, an influential black leader, came to the teenager's defense. Nixon was employed as a railroad sleeping car porter, but his passion was working to advance human rights. A rugged man with a forceful manner and commanding voice, he founded the Montgomery chapter of the National Association for the Advancement of Colored People (NAACP). Nixon was recognized by blacks and whites alike as a powerful presence in the black community, a vital force to be reckoned with. It was said that he knew every white policeman, judge, and government clerk in town, and he was always ready to help anyone in trouble.

18 When Nixon heard about Claudette Colvin's arrest, he got in touch with Clifford Durr, a liberal white attorney in Montgomery. Together they contacted Fred Gray, a twenty-four-year-old black lawyer who agreed to represent Colvin in court. Gray had grown up in Montgomery, attended Alabama State, and gone to Ohio for law school, because Alabama didn't have a law school for blacks. He was one of only two black attorneys in town.

19 After a brief trial in juvenile court, Claudette was found guilty of assault. She was fined and placed on probation in her parents' custody. She had expected to be cleared, and when the judge announced his verdict, she broke into agonized sobs that shook everyone in the crowded courtroom.

20 "The verdict was a bombshell!" Jo Ann Robinson recalled. "Blacks were as near a breaking point as they had ever been."

21 E.D. Nixon and other blacks leaders wanted to take the entire bus segregation issue into federal court. They hoped to demonstrate that segregated buses were illegal under the U.S. Constitution. But first they needed the strongest possible case-the arrest of a black rider who was above reproach, a person of unassailable character and reputation who could withstand the closest scrutiny. Claudette Colvin, Nixon felt, was too young and immature, too prone to emotional outbursts, to serve as standard-bearer for a long and expensive constitutional test case. As Nixon pointed out, she had fought with police, she came from the poorer side of black Montgomery, and it was later rumored that she was pregnant. "I had to be sure I had somebody I could win with...to ask people to give us a half million dollars to fight discrimination on a bus line," Nixon said later.

NOTES

22   In October 1955, several months after Claudette was convicted, Mary Louise Smith, an eighteen-year-old black girl, was arrested when she refused to move to the back of the bus so a white woman could take her seat. "[The driver] asked me to move three times," Smith recalled. "And I refused. I told him, 'I am not going to move out of my seat. I am not going to move anywhere. I got the privilege to sit her like anybody else does.'"

23   Smith's case did not create the furor that the Colvin case did, because Smith chose to plead guilty. She was fined five dollars. Once again, Nixon decided that Smith, like Colvin, wasn't the right person to inspire a battle against bus segregation.

24   Two months later, on December 1, 1955, another black woman boarded a city bus and found an empty seat just behind the white section. She was Rosa Parks.

Excerpted from *Freedom Walkers: The Story of the Montgomery Bus Boycott* by Russell Freedman, published by Holt McDougal.

THINK QUESTIONS

1. Use details from the text to explain why Edwina and Marshall Johnson have trouble with the Montgomery bus laws.

2. Refer to one or more details from the text to explain what Claudette Colvin learns about the difference between Montgomery's segregation laws and actual practice on buses at that time. Base your answer both on evidence that is directly stated and ideas that you infer from clues in the text.

3. Write several sentences explaining how Claudette Colvin hurts her case by struggling with her arresting officers. Support your answer with textual evidence.

4. The Latin root *civis* means "citizen." Using this information and the context from the text, determine the meaning of the word **civics** as it is used in this excerpt from *Freedom Walkers: The Story of the Montgomery Bus Boycott*. Write your definition of *civics* and explain how you got it.

5. The Greek root *polis* means "city" and is also the root for words such as *police*. Use these origins, along with the context clues provided in the passage, to determine the meaning of **policy.** Write your definition of *policy* and tell how you determined the word's meaning.

CLOSE READ

Reread the excerpt from *Freedom Walkers: The Story of the Montgomery Bus Boycott.* As you reread, complete the Focus Questions below. Then use your answers and annotations from the questions to help you complete the Writing Prompt.

FOCUS QUESTIONS

1. Note that Freedman's text begins with the words "It's my constitutional right," a sentence that is repeated in paragraph 12. Why does Freedman structure the text in this way, and how does this repetition contribute to the development of ideas? Highlight evidence from the text and make annotations to explain your analysis.

2. How does paragraph 5 form a transitional bridge between the stories of the Johnson siblings and Claudette Colvin as well as state a main idea of the text? Support your answer with textual evidence and make annotations to explain your analysis.

3. Freedman brings attention to Claudette Colvin's education in paragraphs 6 and 12. How does this repeated reference contribute to the development of ideas in the text? Highlight textual evidence and make annotations to explain your analysis.

4. In paragraph 13, how does Freedman use text structure to connect Colvin's experience to other African Americans? Highlight textual evidence and make annotations to support your analysis.

5. In what ways are Edwina and Marshall Johnson and Claudette Colvin heroes? Highlight textual evidence and make annotations to explain your ideas.

WRITING PROMPT

In this chapter, Russell Freedman informs readers about a sequence of events that preceded the Montgomery bus boycott, and he also makes a connection between the actions of Edwina and Marshall Johnson in 1949, other African American bus riders in Montgomery over the next few years, and Claudette Colvin in 1955. How does each section of the text fit into the overall structure and contribute to Freedman's development of ideas? Use your understanding of informational text structure to analyze the excerpt. Support your writing with textual evidence, including facts, details, and quotations. Use precise vocabulary as appropriate to explain the topic, including words specifically related to the issues and laws of the time.

SUNRISE OVER FALLUJAH

FICTION
Walter Dean Myers
2008

INTRODUCTION

Robin Perry doesn't know exactly why he joined the Army after 9/11, but he knows he is headed to the Mideast to take part in Operation Iraqi Freedom. As part of a unit meant to stabilize the country and interact with the Iraqi people, it isn't long before he realizes that good intentions take a backseat to

"'So what are you doing in Kuwait?' I asked."

 FIRST READ

Excerpt from Chapter 1

1   We left the tent and drifted out into the bright Kuwaiti sun. The intense direct light was always a bit of a shock and I saw guys going for their water bottles. I wasn't sure whether I should drink as much water as possible or try to train myself to drink less.

2   Since Kuwait was right next to Iraq, I thought things would be tense here, but they're not. Our living quarters are in a warehouse area; the mess hall is really good and it even has a coffee shop. There are also fast food places, a theater, and a library that was built after the first Gulf War. After two weeks in the country, I was still trying to get used to the heat and even complaining like everybody else, but down deep this is a little exciting, too. I'm also wondering if there really is going to be a war. There is a huge amount of guys and heavy equipment already here and more being brought in every day.

3   "Hey, Birdy!"

4   I turned around and a tall blonde caught up with me. I'm six-two and we were almost eye to eye when she reached me. I glanced at her name tape. Kennedy.

5   "Say, Birdy, weren't you at Fort Dix?" she asked.

6   "Yeah, and the name is Robin, not Birdy," I said.

7   "Whatever," she said. "I like Birdy better."

8   "Kennedy, I knocked out the last person who got my name wrong," I said.

9   "Really? I'm impressed," she said; a grin spread across her face. "What kind of weapon was she carrying?"

10 Kennedy flipped the sling of her M-16 over her shoulder and **sauntered** off toward the women's quarters.

11 I had come down with measles at Fort Dix, New Jersey, with only two weeks left to go in my **infantry** training cycle. After a week in **isolation** at the hospital I spent three weeks hanging around the dayroom watching television and shooting pool while it was being decided if I would have to repeat the whole cycle again. I ended up with another training group and then received orders to report to the Civil Affairs **detachment** at Camp Doha in Kuwait.

12 I went to dinner in the main mess. The tables actually had flowers and napkins on them and we ate off regular plates instead of the trays we had used at Fort Dix. I grabbed some meat loaf, mashed potatoes, and string beans, and found a table. One of the guys who had been at the meeting with Major Sessions came over and asked if he could join me.

13 "Sure," I said. The guy was about five-seven with smooth brown skin and a round face. Solidly built, he looked like he could take care of himself. But when I saw his **camouflage** do-rag and dark shades I knew he was a little different.

14 "So what you about, man?" he asked.

15 "Same thing everybody else is," I answered, "getting ready to go to war. What are you about?"

16 "I'm about the blues," he answered. "You know, the blues is what's real. Everything else is just messing around waiting until you get back to the blues."

17 "So what are you doing in Kuwait?" I asked. I glanced down at his name tape. It read JONES.

18 "Yeah, I'm Jones," he said. "But everybody back home calls me 'Jonesy.' What I'm doing here is getting some experience, getting to see some stuff, and saving my money so I can open up a blues club. When I get that club going I'm going to play blues guitar six nights a week. Then on Sundays I'll jam with God because me and him is like this."

19 Jones held up two crossed fingers.

20 "Yeah, okay."

21 "Yeah, yeah. Look, you and me got to stick together," he said. "That way I can watch your back and you can watch mine."

22 "Okay."

23   "You play guitar?"

24   "No."

25   "You sing?"

26   "No."

27   Jones looked away and I got the feeling he had already lost interest in watching my back. He talked some more about the club he was going to open. He didn't sound as if he had much of an education, but he seemed sincere about wanting to play his guitar. He said he practiced it at least two hours a day.

28   "Yo, Jones, that's good," I said.

29   "'Jonesy,' you got to call me 'Jonesy,'" he said. "That way I know you looking out."

30   I liked Jonesy even though I wasn't sure what he was talking about sometimes. Like when he asked me if I was a hero.

31   "No," I answered.

32   "You tall—how tall are you?"

33   "Six foot two."

34   "A lot of tall dudes are hero types," Jonesy said. "You go crazy trying to watch their backs. You know what I mean?"

35   "Yeah, but I'm not the hero type," I said.

Excerpted from *Sunrise Over Fallujah* by Walter Dean Myers, published by Scholastic Inc.

THINK QUESTIONS

1. Use details from the text to explain how Kuwait is different from the narrator's expectations.

2. Refer to one or more details from the text to explain how Kennedy uses humor to lighten the conversation with the narrator. Base your answer both on evidence that is directly stated and ideas that you have inferred from clues in the text.

3. Write two or three sentences explaining how the narrator and Jonesy have different attitudes toward their time in Kuwait. Support your answer with textual evidence.

4. Use context to determine the meaning of the word **isolation** as it is used in *Sunrise Over Fallujah*. Write your definition of *isolation* and tell how you determined the word's meaning.

5. Remembering that the prefix *de* often means "opposite of," and that the suffix *ment* forms a noun from a verb, use the context clues provided in the passage to determine the meaning of **detachment.** Write your definition of *detachment* and tell how you determined the word's meaning.

CLOSE READ

Reread the excerpt from *Sunrise Over Fallujah*. As you reread, complete the Focus Questions below. Then use your answers and annotations from the questions to help you complete the Writing Prompt.

 FOCUS QUESTIONS

1. Explain how the author, Walter Dean Myers, develops the narrator's point of view in the first two paragraphs of the excerpt from *Sunrise Over Fallujah*. What tone does Meyers communicate through Robin's comments? Is this tone consistent, and if so, what does the author do to maintain it? Support your answer with textual evidence and make annotations to explain your analysis.

2. In paragraph 11, Robin is isolated in the hospital for measles. What tone does Myers's choice of words establish toward military decision making? Highlight textual evidence and make annotations to explain your analysis.

3. In paragraphs 12 and 13, what does Robin notice about the mess hall and about Jonesy? How do his observations add to what readers already know about Robin and about his point of view on life in a military camp? In paragraph 15, what does Robin's reply tell you about his point of view?

4. In paragraph 16, Jonesy explains that he's "about" the blues, and the characters go on to talk more about the blues and playing music in paragraphs 18 through 28. What tone does the author convey toward the blues through the characters' conversation? What words, phrases, or sentence structures help maintain this tone? Highlight textual evidence and make annotations to support your analysis.

5. In paragraphs 30, 34, and 35 Jonesy and Robin each use the term *hero*. How does Jonesy use the word? How does Robin use the word? Do the two characters define *hero* in the same way? Highlight textual evidence and make annotations to explain your analysis.

WRITING PROMPT

By using a first-person narrator, Walter Dean Myers ensures that readers will experience *Sunrise Over Fallujah* only through what Robin is able to see, hear, think, and observe. How might the story's point of view be different if a different character, Jonesy for example, was the first-person narrator who told the story? How might the tone of the story be different? Using details from the text, write an essay explaining how the excerpt would be different if told from Jonesy's point of view. What might Jonesy notice that would be different from what Robin observes? What would Jonesy's attitude be toward life in the camp? Would he share Robin's excitement or have other feelings? What would Jonesy have to say about Robin himself? Would his point of view on Robin be favorable? Use what you have learned about tone to establish a formal tone in your essay, and maintain it. Use textual evidence to support your ideas.

AN AMERICAN PLAGUE:

THE TRUE AND TERRIFYING STORY OF
THE YELLOW FEVER EPIDEMIC OF 1793

NON-FICTION
Jim Murphy
2003

INTRODUCTION

Thought to have originated in Africa, yellow fever spread to the Americas in the 17th and 18th centuries on trading ships. In 1793, the plague struck inhabitants of quayside neighborhoods in Philadelphia with gruesome and heartbreaking results. Author Jim Murphy takes an unflinching look at the scourge, including the doctors who labored to save the afflicted and discover the causes and cures, the politicians who sought to govern the panicked city,

"...her skin took on the pale-yellow color that gave the disease its name."

 FIRST READ

Excerpt from Chapter 2: All Was Not Right

1 *"8 or 10 persons buried out of Water St. between Race and Arch Sts.; many sick in our neighborhood, and in ye City generally."*
—Elizabeth Drinker, August 21, 1793

2 **Monday, August 19.** It was clear that thirty-three-year-old Catherine LeMaigre was dying, and dying horribly and painfully. Between agonized gasps and groans she muttered that her stomach felt as if it were burning up. Every ten minutes or so her moaning would stop abruptly and she would vomit a foul black bile.

3 Her husband, Peter, called in two neighborhood doctors to save his young wife. One was Dr. Hugh Hodge, whose own daughter had been carried off by the same fever just days before. Hodge had been an army surgeon during the Revolutionary War, and while stubborn and crusty in his ways, he was a respected physician. The other was Dr. John Foulke, who was a fellow of Philadelphia's **prestigious** College of Physicians and a member of the Pennsylvania Hospital board.

4 Hodge and Foulke did what they could for their patient. They gave her cool drinks of barley water and apple water to reduce the fever, and red wine with laudanum to help her rest. Her forehead, face, and arms were washed regularly with damp cloths.

5 Nothing worked, and Catherine LeMaigre's condition worsened. Her pulse slowed, her eyes grew bloodshot, her skin took on the pale-yellow color that gave the disease its name. More black vomit came spewing forth. In desperation, the two physicians sent for their esteemed colleague Dr. Benjamin Rush.

Please note that excerpts and passages in the StudySync® library and this workbook are intended as touchstones to generate interest in an author's work. The excerpts and passages do not substitute for the reading of entire texts, and StudySync® strongly recommends that students seek out and purchase the whole literary or informational work in order to experience it as the author intended. Links to online resellers are available in our digital library. In addition, complete works may be ordered through an authorized reseller by filling out and returning to StudySync® the order form enclosed in this workbook.

Reading & Writing
Companion

33

6   Rush was forty-seven years old and so highly respected that he was often called in by colleagues when they were baffled by a case. His medical training had been extensive, consisting of five years of apprenticeship with the pre-eminent doctor in the United States, John Redman. After this he had gone to Europe to study under the most skilled surgeons and doctors in the western world.

7   He was passionate and outspoken in his beliefs, no matter what the subject. He opposed slavery, felt that alcohol and tobacco should be avoided, urged that the corporal punishment of children be stopped, and thought that the best way to keep a democracy strong was by having universal education. Along with his beliefs went an unimaginable amount of energy. Despite a persistent cough and weak lungs that often left him gasping for air, he worked from early in the morning until late at night—writing letters and papers, visiting patients, rereading the latest medical literature, or attending to any one of a number of institutions and charities he belonged to.

8   Hodge and Foulke told Rush about Catherine LeMaigre's **symptoms** and what they had done to help her. There was nothing much else they could do, Rush said, after the three men left her bedchamber to discuss the case. Rush then noted that in recent days he had seen "an unusual number of bilious fevers, accompanied with symptoms of uncommon malignity." In a grave voice, his seriousness reflected in his intense blue eyes, he added that "all was not right in our city."

9   The two other doctors agreed, and then all three recounted the symptoms they had seen. The sickness began with chills, headache, and a painful aching in the back, arms, and legs. A high fever developed, accompanied by constipation. This stage lasted around three days, and then the fever suddenly broke and the patient seemed to recover.

10 But only for a few short hours.

11 The next stage saw the fever shoot up again. The skin and eyeballs turned yellow, as red blood cells were destroyed, causing the bile pigment bilirubin to accumulate in the body; nose, gums, and intestines began bleeding; and the patient vomited stale, black blood. Finally, the pulse grew weak, the tongue turned a dry brown, and the victim became depressed, confused, and delirious.

12 Rush noted another sign as well: tiny reddish eruptions on the skin. "They appeared chiefly on the arms, but they sometimes extended to the breast." Physicians called these sores petechiae, which is Latin for skin spots, and Rush observed that they "resembled moscheto bites."

13 Hodge then pointed out that the deaths, including his daughter's, had all happened on or near Water Street. Foulke told of other deaths along the street and said he knew the origin of the fevers: the repulsive smell in the air caused by the rotting coffee on Ball's Wharf.

14 The idea that illness was caused by **microscopic organisms,** such as **bacteria** and **viruses,** was not known at the time. Instead, doctors based their medical thinking on the 2,500-year-old Greek humoral theory. This concept stated that good health resulted when body fluids, called humors, were in balance. The humors were phlegm, choler, bile, and blood.

15 Disease arose from an imbalance of these humors—too much of one, not enough of another. Any number of things could cause this condition, such as poor diet, excess drinking, poison, or a dog bite, to name just a few. Even bad news could unsettle the humors and cause illness. So it made sense to Rush, Hodge, and Foulke that the putrid-smelling air could upset people enough to cause an outbreak of violent, fatal fevers.

16 Rush, however, sensed something else. The symptoms he was seeing reminded him of a sickness that had swept through Philadelphia back in 1762, when he was sixteen years old and studying under Dr. Redman. Rush was never shy with his opinions, and standing there in the LeMaigres' parlor, he boldly announced that the disease they now confronted was the dreaded yellow fever.

Excerpted from *An American Plague* by Jim Murphy, published by Clarion Books.

THINK QUESTIONS

1. Use details from the text to describe three symptoms that indicated a patient had yellow fever.

2. Refer to one or more details from the text to explain both the suspected and the true causes of yellow fever. Why was Benjamin Rush suspicious of the suspected cause?

3. Write two or three sentences explaining how Dr. Rush was able to diagnose the yellow fever. Support your answer with textual evidence.

4. The Greek word root *symptoma* means "happening." Use this root, along with the context, to determine the technical meaning of the word **symptoms** as it is used in *An American Plague: The True and Terrifying Story of the Yellow Fever Epidemic of 1793*. Write your definition of *symptoms* and tell how you determined it.

5. The Greek prefix *micro* means "small" and the Greek root *scop* means "to see." Use these word parts along with the context clues provided in the passage to determine the technical meaning of **microscopic.** Write your definition of *microscopic* here and tell how you determined it.

Please note that excerpts and passages in the StudySync® library and this workbook are intended as touchstones to generate interest in an author's work. The excerpts and passages do not substitute for the reading of entire texts, and StudySync® strongly recommends that students seek out and purchase the whole literary or informational work in order to experience it as the author intended. Links to online resellers are available in our digital library. In addition, complete works may be ordered through an authorized reseller by filling out and returning to StudySync® the order form enclosed in this workbook.

Reading & Writing
Companion

35

CLOSE READ

Reread the excerpt from *An American Plague: The True and Terrifying Story of the Yellow Fever Epidemic of 1793.* As you reread, complete the Focus Questions below. Then use your answers and annotations from the questions to help you complete the Writing Prompt.

FOCUS QUESTIONS

1. How do the details of Catherine LeMaigre's illness in paragraphs 2 and 5 connect to the details of Dr. Hodge's daughter's illness in paragraph 3, and the illnesses of other patients in the city in paragraphs 8–13? How do they help convey the central idea of the text? Highlight evidence from the text and make annotations to explain your ideas.

2. What details in paragraphs 4 and 5 cause Drs. Hodge and Foulke to send for Dr. Rush? How does the decision to consult with Dr. Rush prove key in diagnosing Catherine LeMaigre and support the central idea of the text? Support your answer with textual evidence and make annotations to explain your ideas.

3. In paragraphs 14–15, readers may note that the passage describes the medical thinking prevalent during the late 1700s. Identify the key details in the passage. What do they have in common? Use the central idea and key details to summarize this passage. Highlight important details in the text and make annotations to explain your reasoning.

4. What do the ways in which Drs. Hodge and Foulke respond to the mysterious illness of their patient, Catherine LeMaigre, reveal about their character? Highlight details from the text and make annotations to provide evidence for your answer.

5. In what ways is Dr. Rush a hero? Highlight textual evidence and make annotations to explain your ideas.

WRITING PROMPT

Notice that the text says that Dr. Rush "worked from early in the morning until late at night" on a number of tasks, including "writing letters and papers." Physicians often write papers about health-related topics for publication in medical journals. Imagine that you are Dr. Hodge, Dr. Foulke, or Dr. Rush. Summarize for city politicians the health situation in Philadelphia in 1793. What might you say? Write an objective summary introducing the central or main idea and the most important details that support it, such as facts, definitions, and examples. Be sure not to include irrelevant details or your feelings or judgments. Use precise language and specific vocabulary, such as scientific and medical terms, as appropriate in your summary, and include transitions to connect your ideas. Maintain a formal style, and provide a conclusion that follows from the information you present. Support your writing with textual evidence.

CELEBRITIES AS HEROES

NON-FICTION
2015

INTRODUCTION

There is no question that celebrities are frequently idolized as heroes, especially by young people. But do they deserve such admiration? The authors of these two articles have different opinions. One claims that most celebrities are not heroic because they have not done enough to change the world in positive ways. The other argues that many celebrities do qualify as heroes because of their outstanding achievements and influence as role models. Both writers present strong arguments and support their claims with evidence.

"...money, notoriety, and flamboyant behavior don't make someone a hero."

FIRST READ

NOTES

Celebrities as Heroes

Point: Celebrities Should Not Be Idolized as Heroes

1 "Did you read what he said on Twitter? He's my hero!"

2 "Do you know what she did on vacation? She's my hero!"

3 "Did you hear how they finally tracked down the gang in the latest podcast? They're my heroes!"

4 "Did you see what she wore to that awards show? She's my hero!"

5 Today, many people use the word "hero" too lightly. They confuse the word "hero" with the word "celebrity." Right now, almost anyone can be a celebrity just because his or her name or face can be recognized. But money, notoriety, and flamboyant behavior don't make someone a hero. Neither does playing the role of a hero on TV or in the movies. In fact, most celebrities don't deserve to be called heroes because they aren't heroes. They're people who are "celebrities" or "celebrated" for no other reason than because their fame has spread by word of mouth, the press, or social media.

6 What makes a hero? Heroes have been defined as people who have demonstrated admirable qualities such as strength, honesty, courage, and **perseverance,** sometimes at great risk to themselves. They have accomplished something that helped others in some way. For example, by refusing to give up her seat on a bus, Rosa Parks became a hero for civil rights. Her action inspired others to fight for equality in peaceful ways. Firefighters, police officers, soldiers, and regular citizens have often acted heroically when they have saved people from attacks and natural disasters. Heroes can also be individuals who have made a difference in people's lives, such as teachers, parents, coaches, and mentors.

7   When celebrities are **idolized** just because they play heroes in movies and on television or are famous for dangerous or inappropriate publicity stunts, they end up overshadowing real heroes. They may get our attention, but they certainly don't do much to positively change the world. This leaves young people with poor role models and heroes with little substance.

8   Psychologist Abby Aronowitz, Ph.D., says that the media is partly to blame for the hero worship of celebrities. She says that the media devotes a lot of attention to celebrities and little time to reporting on true heroes. However, many who work in the media claim that news about their idols is what people want to watch and read about, and so that's what they give them. Celebrity sells.

9   Dr. Stuart Fischoff of the American Psychological Association says it's normal for people to idolize those who have fame and fortune. "We are **sociologically** preprogrammed to 'follow the leader,'" he says. However, if young people choose to idolize a celebrity who indulges in risky behavior, then they might be inspired to do the same. They may think that if they themselves act like their idol, they too will become famous.

10 While many celebrities love that the media turns them into heroes, other celebrities criticize these false images. They don't want to be heroes. They don't want the pressure of being seen as role models for young fans. They know that their mistakes will be widely reported and will likely upset and disappoint those who idolize them. However, the price of fame is that young fans will continue to idolize celebrity superstars and consider them heroes.

11 Convincing young people that celebrities do not make good role models or heroes will be difficult if there are no real heroes to replace the celebrities. So the media and parents need to focus on real heroes. Many can be found in history. Examples include Martin Luther King Jr., Eleanor Roosevelt, Gandhi, and Abraham Lincoln. There are also many everyday men and women who have acted heroically by facing danger to help people. Even though they have flaws as all humans do, their courage can inspire others. Such heroes will still be heroes long after celebrities are no longer remembered.

Counterpoint: Celebrities Can Be Cultural Heroes

12 After the baseball game is over, young fans line up to get autographs from their favorite players. The player who hit the home run that won the game is greeted with cheers. One fan yells, "You're my hero!"

13 Many actors, singers, and television stars are idolized with the same adoration that many fans show sports stars. They are all famous celebrities, but are they also heroes? Do they deserve or even want such admiration?

14 Society is very quick to sneer at celebrities who are idolized and very ready to say that any contribution a celebrity makes is minor. Many people are **dismissive** of celebrities just because they are celebrities. Yet, there are many celebrities who are true heroes. These individuals may have struggled courageously to reach their goals and made outstanding achievements in their fields—sports, movies, music, fashion—that can inspire others.

15 Striving to be the best one can be at a sport or in science, medicine, or another profession can require extraordinary skill, determination, self-sacrifice, and dedication. Celebrities who set good examples as role models for striving and achieving at the very highest levels in their chosen fields and beyond can at times be considered heroic in their struggle, commitment, and accomplishment.

16 Dr. Eric Hollander at the Mt. Sinai School of Medicine in New York City says "Celebrities can have a positive influence on our lives, with positive messages." This is especially true when fans appreciate a celebrity's abilities and achievements. They may idolize a soccer player's genuine ability to play well and score points in nearly every game. This admiration may lead young fans to work harder when they play soccer because they want to be like their hero.

17 In addition, some celebrities have made outstanding contributions to charitable causes. Paul Newman was called one of the best actors of his time, but he also founded a food company that donates all of its profits to charity. Other celebrities like Derek Jeter have attained greatness in their chosen fields and are also very active in charitable work. Jeter created an organization that helps kids turn away from drugs and alcohol. As a result, celebrities like Derek Jeter have a positive effect on people, especially their young fans, who are inspired to live healthier lives. Helping people is definitely something that heroes do.

18 Because many celebrities deserve admiration for their achievements in or beyond their chosen fields, it's really up to the fans to choose their heroes carefully. Fans need to know what qualities real heroes have and to look for these qualities in the celebrities they are attracted to. They need to ask themselves if they are worshiping celebrities just because these people are famous or because they are true heroes. If fans confuse mere celebrities with real heroes, they rob themselves of good role models. If the only celebrities young people are exposed to do nothing but go to parties, wear expensive clothes, appear on television gossip programs, and act rudely, then that is who will be a major influence on young people.

19 It's also up to the media to pay more attention to celebrities who are true role models. This is not always easy because these celebrities are not necessarily

looking for the media to shine a spotlight on their actions. They are involved in helping refugees, fighting for conservation, or working to improve people's health because these issues are important to them. They aren't doing these things to increase their fame or to be admired as heroes.

20 We all need heroes; people we can look up to and strive to imitate. If we are clear about the qualities we admire, we will be able to find many true role models among that diverse group of people we categorize simply as "celebrities. But the individuals we choose to call our "heroes" can't be just any celebrities. They should be people who, by example or action, are trying to make a difference in other people's lives.

 ## THINK QUESTIONS

1. Cite the "Point" author's main claim and one reason why the author makes the claim. What evidence does the author provide to support this position? Use details from the text to support your answer.

2. Use details from the text to explain the "Counterpoint" author's main claim and one reason why the author makes this claim. What evidence does the author provide to support this position?

3. The "Point" author acknowledges that some celebrities, particularly sports stars, do not want to be heroes or role models, but he or she insists that these desires are irrelevant. Explain the author's position on this issue. Use textual evidence to support your answer.

4. Use context clues from the text to determine the meaning of the word **perseverance** as it is used in "Celebrities as Heroes" Write your definition of *perseverance* here and tell how you determined the word's meaning.

5. Remembering that the Latin root *socio* means "friend or companion" and the suffix *-ology* means "a branch of learning," use the context clues provided in the selection to determine the meaning of **sociologically**. Write your definition of *sociologically* and tell how you determined the word's meaning.

Please note that excerpts and passages in the StudySync® library and this workbook are intended as touchstones to generate interest in an author's work. The excerpts and passages do not substitute for the reading of entire texts, and StudySync® strongly recommends that students seek out and purchase the whole literary or informational work in order to experience it as the author intended. Links to online resellers are available in our digital library. In addition, complete works may be ordered through an authorized reseller by filling out and returning to StudySync® the order form enclosed in this workbook.

Reading & Writing Companion   41

CLOSE READ

Reread the text "Celebrities as Heroes." As you reread, complete the Focus Questions below. Then use your answers and annotations from the questions to help you complete the Writing Prompt.

FOCUS QUESTIONS

1. Review the "Point" author's claim in paragraph 5 of the "Point" section that "most celebrities don't deserve to be called heroes because they aren't heroes." What reason does the author give in the same paragraph for making his or her claim? What evidence is missing to support the word *most* in the claim? Then review the "Counterpoint" author's claim in paragraph 14 of the "Counterpoint" section that "there are many celebrities who are true heroes." What reason does this author give in the same paragraph for making his or her claim? What evidence is missing to support the word *many* in the claim? Highlight textual evidence and make annotations to explain your ideas.

2. In paragraph 7, the "Point" author states that celebrities "end up overshadowing real heroes" and that this "leaves young people with poor role models and heroes with little substance." What evidence does the "Point" author include in paragraph 8 to support this statement? What additional information could the author have included to make his or her argument more effective? Highlight textual evidence and make annotations to support your evaluation.

3. Evaluate the evidence provided by the expert quoted in paragraph 9 of the "Point" section. How well does it support the "Point" author's claim that celebrities should not be considered heroes? Highlight textual evidence and make annotations to support your evaluation.

4. Identify a reason that the "Counterpoint" author provides in paragraph 16 of "Celebrities Can Be Cultural Heroes" to support his or her claim. What evidence supports the reason and claim? Evaluate the strength of the evidence. Highlight textual evidence and make annotations to explain your analysis.

5. Do you agree or disagree with the "Point" author that historical figures, firefighters, police officers, soldiers, teachers, parents, coaches, and mentors are more heroic than most celebrities? Why or why not? Highlight textual evidence and make annotations to explain your ideas.

WRITING PROMPT

The "Point" and "Counterpoint" authors offer two points of view regarding whether celebrities are heroes. Both offer reasons and evidence to support their claims. If you trace and evaluate the argument of each author, which author is most convincing? Which author most effectively uses reasons and evidence to support his or her claim? Is each claim fully supported by reasons and evidence? If not, which aspect of the particular claim remains unsupported? Use your understanding of purpose and point of view as you evaluate the argument in each passage. Support your opinion with textual evidence.

THE EDUCATION OF GEORGE WASHINGTON:

HOW A FORGOTTEN BOOK SHAPED THE CHARACTER OF A HERO

NON-FICTION
Austin Washington
2014

INTRODUCTION

The Education of George Washington, a biography of the American hero written by his great-nephew Austin Washington, offers a lively and humorous account of Washington's life. The book focuses on how a forgotten 200-year-old text and other experiences helped shape Washington into a man who represents honor, courage, and integrity. In the excerpt, Washington and his troops face a desperate situation at Valley Forge, and receive assistance from Baron von Steuben of the Prussian army.

"Dysentery, typhoid, consumption, pneumonia, jaundice, etc., all had their way with the troops."

 FIRST READ

Excerpt from Chapter Eleven: Valley Forge

1   Most of us have heard about the hard, cold winter at Valley Forge. The bloody feet in the snow and all the rest.

2   For those of you for whom the details are a bit hazy, war was a summer thing in those days. No major battles were expected to be fought in the off season. Both armies would hunker down for the winter. Valley Forge, Pennsylvania, was selected as the winter home for the twelve thousand or so soldiers directly under George's control in the fall of 1777, a year after the crossing of the Delaware had given the Americans their first unambiguous victory.

3   Although the first months of Valley Forge were a hellish struggle—if hell can be freezing, that is—there are no contemporary images of the cadaverous survivors to remind us of the horror.

4   The most famous image, which is both fictional and trite, is a painting made 198 years after the (non) incident, depicting George Washington, fully clothed and shod (as he of course would have been), praying alone in the snow (as he never did). For those of a less Norman Rockwellesque frame of mind—it was actually a guy named Friberg who made that particularly falsely iconic, Rockwellesque image—Valley Forge is seen most often as a metaphor for the entire revolutionary struggle: against impossible odds, impossibly undersupplied troops suffered and sacrificed with no realistic hope in sight.

5   But they soldiered on.

6   Without any evocative images to remind us, though, the true horror is often forgotten. As fall turned into winter in 1777, two-thirds of the twelve thousand soldiers camped in Valley Forge still had no shoes. No shoes! At one point, a third were listed as unfit for duty—well, four thousand or so, which was more

than a third once you subtract the twenty-five hundred who had died by the spring from the horrific diseases that sliced through the camp, all of them untreatable at the time and most of them contagious.

7 Dysentery, typhoid, consumption, pneumonia, jaundice, etc., all had their way with the troops. It didn't help that the conditions were horrifyingly unsanitary by modern standards (and by contemporaneous Prussian standards, but we'll get to that in a minute). Nor, of course, did the freezing cold offer any comfort.

8 In short, George Washington's army was in desperate conditions—even more desperate than the circumstances of the Duke of Schonberg's army that, as George had read in the Panegyrick, once suffered "an incredible scarcity of all things; and the rage of Hunger, more cruel than that of the Sword. . . weaken'd below by Mortal Diseases; consum'd from within with want; and fac'd without, with a numerous Army. . . ." This was warfare in the era before modern technology, when the difference between defeat and victory wasn't who had stealth fighters and bunker-busting bombs, but who was best able to rise above hunger and disease to fight on.

9 Lack of adequate shelter, at least at first, contributed to the misery, suffering, and disease of George's men. Hobbit homes would have been a step up from the accommodations originally available at Valley Forge. Malnutrition didn't help. The soldiers survived, at times, on nothing but "fire bread," made from flour, melted snow, and nothing else. Occasionally their diet would be supplemented by fallen animals, which were butchered where they fell. They would let what little might remain rot, although the rotting was, as some small consolation, limited by the cold.

10 They relieved themselves where they were, the germ theory of disease being a century in the future. The cold therefore prevented at least some incidents of illness by freezing things that might otherwise putrefy.

11 But the cold also killed throughout the winter.

12 This suffering, **epitomized** by shoeless soldiers' bloody footprints in the snow, is the darkest image that comes to us from that winter at Valley Forge, Pennsylvania.

13 What most people don't see is why and how the American soldiers—those who survived, that is—overcame all of this. They emerged tougher, stronger, and better, rather than weaker, crippled, and dispirited, as would surely have been the case without the entrance, towards the end of that winter, of someone almost more **prototypically** American—or at least more self-made— than George Washington.

14 Lieutenant General Friedrich Wilhelm Rudolf Gerhard Augustin Baron von Steuben—Baron von Steuben for short—was little of what his name would suggest. For one, he seems to have been a self-appointed baron. Then again, Michael Jackson was a self-anointed King (of Pop). Self-anointing, rather than inheriting titles, seems to be the American fashion, so von Steuben fit right in.

15 Nor, going a little deeper, had he been a lieutenant general in the Prussian army, as the Americans believed. He had risen to the rank of major there and later been given the honorary title of lieutenant general in a prince's court, after he had been downsized out of the Prussian army. Von Steuben was, though, **indisputably** a Friedrich, a Wilhelm, a Rudolf, and a Gerhard, all at once, which is more than most people can say for themselves.

16 Von Steuben is often given short shrift for his inflated credentials, but as he was to make his biggest mark in a land in which no one of importance had any credentials—the most notable of all, such as Washington and Benjamin Franklin, lacking even university degrees—an observer might ask a big, historical so what? Okay, he was a captain and then major, never a general in the Prussian army, but it *was* the Prussian *army*, widely considered the best in Europe. And he wasn't just any staff officer, he had been aide-de-camp to the King of Prussia. The King!

17 Von Steuben was even one of thirteen officers selected for a *Spezialklasse der Kriegskunst,* a kind of warfare class conducted by the King. Presumably the baron—or whatever he was—was chosen for that class by the King himself. As von Steuben didn't speak English very well, the whole "lieutenant general in the Prussian army" thing was very possibly a misunderstanding. Meanwhile the title, if incorrect, did arguably convey his background and skill in a kind of shorthand.

18 Anyway, the somewhat inflated background is what Benjamin Franklin conveyed in a letter he wrote to George Washington (who was later to repeat the characterization), when Franklin was in Europe scouting out potential officers.

19 If the inflated military rank was of the same provenance as the "baron" title—which might, to be fair, have been the fault of faulty genealogical work by his father, not deliberate **mendacity** on the part of either von Steuben fils or père—or if they were both puffery, we still won the war, which we might not have done otherwise.

20 Von Steuben proved himself by his actions, just as George Washington and Benjamin Franklin (and all great Americans since) have done.

21 Von Steuben, after all, started his life in a land where a "baron" title would open up vistas—promotions, positions at court—that would be otherwise

NOTES

closed to him. He then came to a land where a convenient conflation of ranks advanced his career to the level where his skills and talents naturally should have placed him. We are here today, most would agree, because von Steuben overcame the limitations of his birth by the only means reasonably available, puffery. It sounds unpleasant. But it worked.

22 Von Steuben, who loved the pomp of the army as much as anything else, traveled to America, somewhat exotically, not with a wife but with a greyhound. Von Steuben's dog, whether by nature or nurture, had learned to howl when someone sang out of tune (but to wag his tail when the singing was in tune). The dog's short-legged, jowly master wore "a splendid medal of gold and diamonds" on his chest, which was the outward sign of an honorary knighthood. How could he be ignored?

23 George Washington rode out especially to meet him, and was, if not instantly taken, then very soon impressed. The "baron" may have been **eccentric**, but then geniuses often are, aren't they? He was, as George was soon to see, exactly the man George needed to supply the order and discipline the American army so desperately needed.

24 Possibly von Steuben's most important contribution to the American army—don't laugh, it saved countless lives—was putting the latrines *down* hill from where the soldiers lived. Sounds obvious, doesn't it? The Americans hadn't thought of it.

25 Oh, and he also came up with the idea of the latrines themselves. Someone had to suggest them, and that someone was the little "baron" himself. He had picked up his ideas in Germany, where latrines were standard issue.

26 Despite his Prussian background, von Steuben was American enough to particularly point out what he found a refreshing—if at first infuriating—difference between American soldiers and their European counterparts. Ultimately, the difference in American soldiers was the spirit of the Revolution, itself, its *raison d'etre*. Or, as Von Steuben put it, "The genius"—that is, the inherent spirit—"of this nation is not in the least to be compared with the Prussians, the Austrians, or French." While you could say to a European soldier, "'Do this,' and he doeth it," in America, von Steuben discovered, "I am obliged to say, 'This is the reason why you ought to do that,' and then he does it."

27 In other words, Americans thought for themselves. Even the common soldiers didn't let themselves be pushed around.

THINK QUESTIONS

1. Use details from the text to write two or three sentences describing the conditions at Valley Forge.

2. Write two or three sentences explaining whom the author credits for not only the survival but the toughness and strength of the American soldiers at Valley Forge. Support your answer with textual evidence.

3. Refer to one or more details from the text to explain what Baron von Steuben credits for not only the soldiers' survival at Valley Forge but ultimately for the American victory in the war— both from ideas that are directly stated and ideas that you have inferred from clues in the text.

4. Use context to determine the meaning of the word **indisputably** as it is used in *The Education of George Washington: How a Forgotten Book Shaped the Character of a Hero.* Write your definition of *indisputably* and tell how you determined the word's meaning. How might you pronounce this word? Use a dictionary to confirm the word's precise meaning and pronunciation.

5. Remembering that the prefix *proto-* means "original" and the suffix *-ly* means "in a particular manner," use the context clues provided in the passage to determine the meaning of **prototypically,** and make an inference about its pronunciation. Write your definition of *prototypically* and tell how you determined the word's meaning. Then, check your definition and pronunciation in a dictionary.

CLOSE READ

Reread the excerpt from *The Education of George Washington: How a Forgotten Book Shaped the Character of a Hero.* As you reread, complete the Focus Questions below. Then use your answers and annotations from the questions to help you complete the Writing Prompt.

FOCUS QUESTIONS

1. What point does Austin Washington make in paragraph 3 that helps you understand his point of view about the Friberg painting in paragraph 4? Highlight textual evidence and use the annotation tool to explain your reasoning.

2. Highlight examples of personification used in paragraph 8. Then use the annotation tool to explain how the personification helps you understand what is being described.

3. In paragraphs 4, 8, and 26, how does the author convey his point of view regarding the spirit of the American soldiers at Valley Forge? Highlight textual evidence and make annotations to explain your analysis.

4. In paragraph 13, the author suggests that Baron von Steuben is the perfect person to lead American soldiers in the Revolutionary War because he is "self-made." Highlight textual evidence and make annotations to explain Washington's point of view.

5. According to the author's point of view, in what ways is von Steuben a hero? Highlight textual evidence and make annotations to explain your evaluation.

WRITING PROMPT

In *The Education of George Washington: How a Forgotten Book Shaped the Character of a Hero,* how effectively does the author, Austin Washington, convey his point of view regarding the events at Valley Forge and the role of Baron von Steuben in the American war effort? How do both the presentation of facts and details, as well as the use of figurative language and personification, support the author's point of view? Do you find the author's point of view convincing? Why or why not? How clear and convincing are the reasons and evidence provided by the author? Cite specific evidence from the text to support your own claim or claims in your writing.

Please note that excerpts and passages in the StudySync® library and this workbook are intended as touchstones to generate interest in an author's work. The excerpts and passages do not substitute for the reading of entire texts, and StudySync® strongly recommends that students seek out and purchase the whole literary or informational work in order to experience it as the author intended. Links to online resellers are available in our digital library. In addition, complete works may be ordered through an authorized reseller by filling out and returning to StudySync® the order form enclosed in this workbook.

Reading & Writing Companion   49

ELEANOR ROOSEVELT:
A LIFE OF DISCOVERY

NON-FICTION
Russell Freedman
1993

INTRODUCTION

Initially reluctant to be a president's wife, "poor little rich girl" Eleanor Roosevelt rose to the challenge. Bright, energetic and courageous, she became the most celebrated and admired First Lady the White House had ever known. As an invaluable researcher for her husband during the years of the Great Depression, and later a representative of the United Nations, Eleanor raised the bar of possibilities for all First Ladies who followed her.

"She dreaded the prospect of living in the White House."

 FIRST READ

Excerpt from Chapter One: First Lady

1   Eleanor Roosevelt never wanted to be a president's wife. When her husband Franklin won his campaign for the presidency in 1932, she felt deeply troubled. She dreaded the prospect of living in the White House.

2   Proud of her accomplishments as a teacher, a writer, and a political power in her own right, she feared that she would have to give up her hard-won independence in Washington. As First Lady, she would have no life of her own. Like other presidential wives before her, she would be assigned the traditional role of official White House hostess, with little to do but greet guests at receptions and preside over formal state dinners.

3   "From the personal standpoint, I did not want my husband to be president," she later confessed. "It was pure selfishness on my part, and I never mentioned my feelings on the subject to him."

4   Mrs. Roosevelt did her duty. During her years in the White House, the executive mansion bustled with visitors at teas, receptions, and dinners. At the same time, however, she cast her fears aside and seized the opportunity to transform the role of America's First Lady. Encouraged by her friends, she became the first wife of a president to have a public life and career.

5   Americans had never seen a First Lady like her. She was the first to open the White House door to reporters and hold on-the-record press conferences, the first to drive her own car, to travel by plane, and to make many official trips by herself. "My missus goes where she wants to!" the president boasted.

6   She was the first president's wife to earn her own money by writing, lecturing, and broadcasting. Her earnings usually topped the president's salary. She gave most of the money to charity.

Please note that excerpts and passages in the StudySync® library and this workbook are intended as touchstones to generate interest in an author's work. The excerpts and passages do not substitute for the reading of entire texts, and StudySync® strongly recommends that students seek out and purchase the whole literary or informational work in order to experience it as the author intended. Links to online resellers are available in our digital library. In addition, complete works may be ordered through an authorized reseller by filling out and returning to StudySync® the order form enclosed in this workbook.

Reading & Writing Companion   **51**

7   When she insisted on her right to take drives by herself, without a chauffeur or a police escort, the Secret Service, worried about her safety, gave her a pistol and begged her to carry it with her. "I [took] it and learned how to use it," she told readers of her popular newspaper column. "I do not mean by this that I am an expert shot. I only wish I were. . . . My opportunities for shooting have been far and few between, but if the necessity arose, I do know how to use a pistol."

8   She had come a long way since her days as an obedient society matron, and, before then, a **timid** child who was "always afraid of something." By her own account, she had been an "ugly duckling" whose mother told her, "You have no looks, so see to it that you have manners." Before she was ten, both of her unhappy parents were dead. She grew up in a time and place where a woman's life was ruled by her husband's interests and needs, and dominated by the domestic duties of wife and mother. "It was not until I reached middle age," she wrote, "that I had the courage to develop interests of my own, outside of my duties to my family."

9   Eleanor Roosevelt lived in the White House during the Great Depression and the Second World War. In her endless travels through America, she served as a fact-finder and trouble-shooter for her husband and an impassioned publicist for her own views about social justice and world peace. She wanted people to feel that their government cared about them. After Franklin Roosevelt's death, she became a major force at the United Nations, where her efforts on behalf of human rights earned her the title, First Lady of the World.

10 People meeting her for the first time often were startled by how "unjustly" the camera treated her. Photographs had not prepared them for her warmth and dignity and **poise.** An unusually tall woman, she moved with the grace of an athlete, and when she walked into a room, the air seemed charged with her **vibrancy.** "No one seeing her could fail to be moved," said her friend Martha Gellhorn. "She gave off light, I cannot explain it better."

11 For thirty years from the time she entered the White House until her death in 1962, Eleanor Roosevelt was the most famous and at times the most **influential** woman in the world. And yet those who knew her best were most impressed by her simplicity, by her total lack of **self-importance**.

12 "About the only value the story of my life may have," she wrote, "is to show that one can, even without any particular gifts, overcome obstacles that seem insurmountable if one is willing to face the fact that they must be overcome; that, in spite of timidity and fear, in spite of a lack of special talents, one can find a way to live widely and fully."

Reading & Writing Companion

Excerpted from *Eleanor Roosevelt: A Life of Discovery* by Russell Freedman, published by Clarion Books.

 THINK QUESTIONS

1. Use details from the text to write two or three sentences describing how Eleanor Roosevelt expected her life to change when she became First Lady.

2. Write two or three sentences explaining how Eleanor Roosevelt both fulfilled the traditional duties of the First Lady and transformed the role. Support your answer with textual evidence.

3. Refer to one or more details from the text to explain how Eleanor Roosevelt transformed from an "ugly" child to a beautiful adult—both from ideas that are directly stated and ideas that you infer from clues in the text.

4. Use context to determine the meaning of the word **timid** as it is used in *Eleanor Roosevelt: A Life of Discovery*. Write your definition of *timid* and tell how you determined the word's meaning. Then, use a dictionary to check your inferred meaning. Does the dictionary meaning change your understanding of the word?

5. Use context to determine the meaning of the word **poise** as it is used in *Eleanor Roosevelt: A Life of Discovery*. Write your definition of *poise* and tell how you determined it. Then, check your meaning in a dictionary or other reference work. Was your inferred meaning accurate?

CLOSE READ

Reread the excerpt from *Eleanor Roosevelt: A Life of Discovery.* As you reread, complete the Focus Questions below. Then use your answers and annotations from the questions to help you complete the Writing Prompt.

FOCUS QUESTIONS

1. In paragraphs 3, 7, 8, and 12, Freedman quotes Eleanor Roosevelt. What might be Freedman's purpose for doing so? Highlight textual evidence and make annotations to explain your analysis.

2. In paragraphs 5 and 10, Freedman quotes others speaking about Eleanor Roosevelt. What might be his purpose for doing so? Support your response with textual evidence and make annotations to explain your analysis.

3. In paragraph 8, the author uses the phrase "ugly duckling" to describe Eleanor Roosevelt as a child. What does the phrase mean? Is it an appropriate description of Roosevelt? Why or why not? What purpose does the author have for including this detail? Highlight your textual evidence and make annotations to explain your analysis.

4. In paragraph 8, Freedman describes Eleanor Roosevelt as "an obedient society matron." In paragraph 9, she is "First Lady of the World." Discuss Freedman's use of the words "matron," and "lady. How does the connotative meaning of each word affect Freedman's description of Roosevelt? Highlight textual evidence and make annotations to support your analysis.

5. In what ways is Eleanor Roosevelt a hero? Highlight textual evidence and make annotations to support your answer.

WRITING PROMPT

Russell Freedman subtitles his biographical portrait of Eleanor Roosevelt "a life of discovery." What does Freedman suggest Eleanor Roosevelt discovered about herself over the course of a lifetime, and what impact do you think her process of self-discovery had on America and the world? Looking to the excerpt from Chapter One, introduce a claim about what Roosevelt discovered about herself, and why Freedman chose to write not just about discovery but also about self-discovery. Support your claim with clear reasons and relevant evidence from the text, including facts, details, and quotations. Organize your information logically and use transitions as needed to clarify relationships among your claim, reasons, and evidence.

ELEANOR ROOSEVELT AND MARIAN ANDERSON

NON-FICTION

Franklin D. Roosevelt Presidential
Library and Museum
2014

INTRODUCTION

Eleanor Roosevelt, First Lady of the United States for 12 years, was an outspoken advocate for social justice. Like many women of her class and background, she belonged to the Daughters of the American Revolution, known as the DAR, a women's organization founded in the nineteenth century to promote American patriotism. Roosevelt's DAR membership came into sharp conflict with her ideals in 1939 when the DAR refused to allow world famous opera singer Marian Anderson to sing in Constitution Hall because Anderson was African American. This web feature by the staff of the FDR Museum and Library describes how Roosevelt protested the decision, and the impact her actions had on racial

"To remain as a member implies approval of that action, therefore I am resigning."

FIRST READ

Eleanor Roosevelt first met African American **contralto** opera singer Marian Anderson in 1935 when the singer was invited to perform at the White House.

1   Ms. Anderson had performed throughout Europe to great praise, and after the White House concert the singer focused her attentions on a lengthy concert tour of the United States. Beginning in 1936, Anderson sang an annual concert to benefit the Howard University School of Music in Washington, DC. These benefit concerts were so successful that each year larger and larger **venues** had to be found.

2   In January 1939, Howard University petitioned the Daughters of the American Revolution (DAR) to use its Washington, DC auditorium called Constitution Hall for a concert to be scheduled over Easter weekend that year. Constitution Hall was built in the late 1920s to house the DAR's national headquarters and host its annual conventions. It seated 4,000 people, and was the largest auditorium in the capital. As such, it was the center of the city's fine arts and music events universe.

3   However, in 1939, Washington, DC was still a racially segregated city, and the DAR was an all-white heritage association that promoted an aggressive form of American patriotism. As part of the original funding arrangements for Constitution Hall, major donors had insisted that only whites could perform on stage. This unwritten white-performers-only policy was enforced against African American singer/actor Paul Robeson in 1930. Additionally, blacks who attended events there were seated in a segregated section of the Hall.

4   The organizers of Marian Anderson's 1939 concert hoped that Anderson's fame and reputation would encourage the DAR to make an exception to its restrictive policy. But the request was denied anyway, and despite pressure from the press, other great artists, politicians, and a new organization called

the Marian Anderson Citizens Committee (MACC), the DAR held fast and continued to deny Anderson use of the Hall.

5 As the controversy grew, First Lady Eleanor Roosevelt carefully weighed the most effective manner to protest the DAR's decision. Mrs. Roosevelt had been issued a DAR membership card only after the 1932 election swept her husband Franklin Roosevelt into the presidency. As such, she was not an active member of the DAR. She initially chose not to challenge the DAR directly because, as she explained, the group considered her to be "too radical" and "this situation is so bad that plenty of people will come out against it."

6 Rather, Mrs. Roosevelt first led by **enlightened** example. She agreed to present the Spingarn Medal to Marian Anderson at the upcoming national convention of the National Association for the Advancement of Colored People (NAACP). And she invited Anderson to again perform at the White House, this time for the King and Queen of England when they came to the United States later in the year. But as the weeks went on, Mrs. Roosevelt grew increasingly frustrated that more active DAR members than she were not challenging the group's policy.

Roosevelt Resigns from the DAR

7 On February 26, 1939, Mrs. Roosevelt submitted her letter of **resignation** to the DAR president, declaring that the organization had "set an example which seems to me unfortunate" and that the DAR had "an opportunity to lead in an enlightened way" but had "failed to do so." That same day, she sent a telegram to an officer of the Marian Anderson Citizens Committee publicly expressing for the first time her disappointment that Anderson was being denied a concert venue.

8 On February 27, Mrs. Roosevelt addressed the issue in her *My Day* column, published in newspapers across the country. Without mentioning the DAR or Anderson by name, Mrs. Roosevelt couched her decision in terms everyone could understand: whether one should resign from an organization you disagree with or remain and try to change it from within. Mrs. Roosevelt told her readers that in this situation, "To remain as a member implies approval of that action, therefore I am resigning."

Groundbreaking 1939 Lincoln Memorial Concert

9 Mrs. Roosevelt's resignation thrust the Marian Anderson concert, the DAR, and the subject of racism to the center of national attention. As word of her resignation spread, Mrs. Roosevelt and others quietly worked behind the scenes promoting the idea for an outdoor concert at the Lincoln Memorial, a symbolic site on the National Mall overseen by the Department of the Interior.

Please note that excerpts and passages in the StudySync® library and this workbook are intended as touchstones to generate interest in an author's work. The excerpts and passages do not substitute for the reading of entire texts, and StudySync® strongly recommends that students seek out and purchase the whole literary or informational work in order to experience it as the author intended. Links to online resellers are available in our digital library. In addition, complete works may be ordered through an authorized reseller by filling out and returning to StudySync® the order form enclosed in this workbook.

Reading & Writing Companion 57

10   Interior Secretary Harold Ickes, himself a past president of the Chicago NAACP, was excited about such a display of democracy, and he met with President Roosevelt to obtain his approval. After the President gave his assent, Ickes announced on March 30th that Marian Anderson would perform at the Lincoln Memorial on Easter Sunday.

11   Fearing that she might upstage Anderson's triumphant moment, Mrs. Roosevelt chose not to be publicly associated with the sponsorship of the concert. Indeed, she did not even attend, citing the burdens of a nationwide lecture tour and the forthcoming birth of a grandchild. However, she and others lobbied the various radio networks to broadcast the concert to the nation.

12   On April 9th, seventy-five thousand people, including dignitaries and average citizens, attended the outdoor concert. It was as diverse a crowd as anyone had seen—black, white, old, and young—dressed in their Sunday finest. Hundreds of thousands more heard the concert over the radio. After being introduced by Secretary Ickes who declared that "Genius knows no color line," Ms. Anderson opened her concert with *America*. The operatic first half of the program concluded with *Ave Maria*. After a short intermission, she then sang a selection of spirituals familiar to the African American members of her audience. And with tears in her eyes, Marian Anderson closed the concert with an encore, *Nobody Knows the Trouble I've Seen*.

13   The DAR's refusal to grant Marian Anderson the use of Constitution Hall, Eleanor Roosevelt's resignation from the DAR in protest, and the resulting concert at the Lincoln Memorial combined into a **watershed** moment in civil rights history, bringing national attention to the country's color barrier as no other event had previously done.

14   Mrs. Roosevelt and Marian Anderson remained friends for the rest of Mrs. Roosevelt's life. Marian Anderson continued to sing in venues around the world, including singing the National Anthem at President Kennedy's inauguration in 1961. She died in 1993 at the age of 96.

"Eleanor Roosevelt and Marian Anderson", Franklin D. Roosevelt Presidential Library and Museum, http://www.fdrlibrary.marist.edu/

THINK QUESTIONS

1. Refer to one or more details from the text to explain why organizers at Howard University wanted to use Constitution Hall as a venue for Marian Anderson's annual benefit concert.

2. Use details from the text to write two or three sentences explaining why the Daughters of the American Revolution refused to allow Marian Anderson to perform at Constitution Hall.

3. Explain the strategies that Eleanor Roosevelt used to support Marian Anderson and bring national attention to the country's color barrier. Support your answer by citing textual evidence and making inferences.

4. Use context to determine the meaning of the word **venues** as it is used in "Eleanor Roosevelt and Marian Anderson." Write your definition of *venues* and tell how you determined the word's meaning. Then use a dictionary to determine the precise definition and pronunciation of the word.

5. Use context clues provided in the passage to determine the meaning of the word **enlightened**. Write your definition of *enlightened* and tell how you determined the word's meaning. Then use a dictionary to determine the precise definition and pronunciation of the word.

Please note that excerpts and passages in the StudySync® library and this workbook are intended as touchstones to generate interest in an author's work. The excerpts and passages do not substitute for the reading of entire texts, and StudySync® strongly recommends that students seek out and purchase the whole literary or informational work in order to experience it as the author intended. Links to online resellers are available in our digital library. In addition, complete works may be ordered through an authorized reseller by filling out and returning to StudySync® the order form enclosed in this workbook.

Reading & Writing Companion 59

CLOSE READ

Reread the text "Eleanor Roosevelt and Marian Anderson." As you read, complete the Focus Questions below. Then use your answers and annotations from the questions to help you complete the Writing Prompt.

FOCUS QUESTIONS

Questions 1, 2, and 4 ask you to use documents located on the web. Ask your teacher for URLs to find these documents.

1. Reread paragraphs 5–7 of "Eleanor Roosevelt and Marian Anderson" and reread Eleanor Roosevelt's DAR resignation letter. Compare and contrast Roosevelt's response to the event as described in both media. How does each medium inform the other? Highlight textual evidence in paragraph 5 through 7 and annotate ideas from the letter to show the development of your understanding.

2. Read Mrs. Roosevelt's newspaper column "My Day". How does the column illustrate the claim that the article makes in paragraph 8. "Mrs. Roosevelt couched her decision in terms everyone could understand"? What information do you learn from the column about Mrs. Roosevelt's persuasive techniques? Highlight textual evidence in paragraph 8 and annotate ideas from the column to show the development of your understanding of enlightened leadership.

3. What additional information can a reader gain about Eleanor Roosevelt's character from reading about her decision to resign from the DAR in paragraphs 3 and 4 of the "My Day" column that can't be gained from the article? Highlight textual evidence and make annotations to show your understanding.

4. View the video from the Lincoln Memorial concert. Compare the video to the details in the article about the event. As a reader, what did you visualize about the scene? How did this visualization compare with what you viewed in the video? How does viewing the video contribute to your understanding of the event you read about in the text? Highlight textual evidence in paragraph 12 and annotate ideas from the video to support your ideas.

5. In what ways are Eleanor Roosevelt and Marian Anderson heroes? Highlight textual evidence and make annotations to explain your ideas.

WRITING PROMPT

By integrating the information presented in the primary and secondary sources as well as the audio file, you may develop a coherent understanding of Eleanor Roosevelt's resignation from the DAR and the events that followed. Compare and contrast the secondary authors' presentation of events with the primary sources from Roosevelt herself. Which details are emphasized or absent in each medium? What are the possible reasons behind these choices? How does each source contribute to your understanding of the issue? Support your writing with textual evidence.

MY FATHER IS A SIMPLE MAN

POETRY
Luis Omar Salinas
1987

INTRODUCTION

Luis Omar Salinas was a highly regarded Mexican American poet. Considered one of the founding founders of Chicano poetry in America, Salinas worked alongside other well-known poets like Gary Soto to produce works that have inspired generations of Chicanos. In the words of Soto, Salinas possessed "a powerful imagination, a sensitivity to the world, and an intuitive feel for handling language." In "My Father Is a Simple Man," which comes from Salinas's work, *The Sadness of Days: Selected and New Poems*, the speaker of the poem honors a

"He has taken me on this journey and it's been lifelong."

FIRST READ

1 I walk to town with my father
2 to buy a newspaper. He walks slower
3 than I do so I must slow up.
4 The street is filled with children.
5 We argue about the price of **pomegranates.** I convince
6 him it is the fruit of **scholars.**
7 He has taken me on this journey
8 and it's been lifelong.
9 He's sure I'll be healthy
10 so long as I eat more oranges,
11 and tells me the orange
12 has seeds and so is **perpetual;**
13 and we too will come back
14 like the orange trees.
15 I ask him what he thinks
16 about death and he says
17 he will gladly face it when
18 it comes but won't jump
19 out in front of a car.
20 I'd gladly give my life
21 for this man with a sixth
22 grade education, whose kindness
23 and patience are true. . .
24 The truth of it is, he's the scholar,
25 and when the bitter-hard reality
26 comes at me like a punishing
27 evil stranger, I can always
28 remember that here was a man
29 who was a worker and provider,
30 who learned the simple facts
31 in life and lived by them,

Please note that excerpts and passages in the StudySync® library and this workbook are intended as touchstones to generate interest in an author's work. The excerpts and passages do not substitute for the reading of entire texts, and StudySync® strongly recommends that students seek out and purchase the whole literary or informational work in order to experience it as the author intended. Links to online resellers are available in our digital library. In addition, complete works may be ordered through an authorized reseller by filling out and returning to StudySync® the order form enclosed in this workbook.

Reading & Writing
Companion

63

32　who held no **pretense.**
33　And when he leaves without
34　benefit of **fanfare** or applause
35　I shall have learned what little
36　there is about greatness.

"My Father Is a Simple Man" is reprinted with permission from the publisher of "The Sadness of Days: Selected and New Poems" by Luis Omar Salinas (© 1987 Arte Público Press—University of Houston).

 THINK QUESTIONS

1. Refer to one or more details from the text to explain the disagreement between the speaker and his father over fruit. Base your answer both on evidence that is directly stated and ideas that you infer from clues in the text.

2. Use textual evidence to write three or four sentences that establish the father's age.

3. Use details from the text to explain how the speaker's use of the word *scholar* changes between lines 6 and 24.

4. Use context to determine the meaning of the word **perpetual** as it is used in "My Father Is a Simple Man." Write your definition of *perpetual* and tell how you determined the word's meaning.

5. The French word *fanfarer* means "to blow trumpets." Use this root meaning and the context clues provided in the passage to determine the meaning of **fanfare.** Write your definition of *fanfare* and tell how you determined the word's meaning.

CLOSE READ

Reread the poem "My Father Is a Simple Man." As you reread, complete the Focus Questions below. Then use your answers and annotations from the questions to help you complete the Writing Prompt.

FOCUS QUESTIONS

1. In lines 11–12, 15–19, 20, and 33, how does the speaker make death one theme of the poem? What is his message regarding death? Highlight evidence from the text and make annotations to explain your analysis.

2. In lines 1 and 29, how does the speaker make family one theme of the poem? What is his message regarding family? Support your answer with textual evidence and make annotations to explain your analysis.

3. Note that Salinas structures his poem as a single free verse stanza. Remember that free verse describes poetry that does not rhyme or have a regular rhythm or meter. How does this poetic structure contribute to the development of the poem's theme? Highlight your textual evidence and make annotations to explain your analysis.

4. Listen to the audio reading of lines 20 through 26. How does the speaker use pacing, guided by the ellipsis in the print text, to show a new understanding of his father? Highlight textual evidence in the lines and annotate ideas from the audio recording to show the development of your understanding of media techniques.

5. In what ways is the speaker's father a hero? Highlight textual evidence and make annotations to explain your ideas.

6. Use your understanding of the theme of the poem to summarize the speaker's feelings about his father. Highlight textual evidence and make annotations to explain your ideas.

WRITING PROMPT

The poem "My Father Is a Simple Man" ends with the speaker saying that he will "have learned what little/ there is about greatness" when his father dies. What has the speaker learned about greatness from his father? Do you agree with the speaker that greatness is a topic about which there is "little" to learn? Why or why not? Use your understanding of theme and poetic structure to analyze the message of the poem. Support the ideas you express in your response to the literature with textual evidence, including details, descriptions, and quotations from the poem.

Please note that excerpts and passages in the StudySync® library and this workbook are intended as touchstones to generate interest in an author's work. The excerpts and passages do not substitute for the reading of entire texts, and StudySync® strongly recommends that students seek out and purchase the whole literary or informational work in order to experience it as the author intended. Links to online resellers are available in our digital library. In addition, complete works may be ordered through an authorized reseller by filling out and returning to StudySync® the order form enclosed in this workbook.

Reading & Writing Companion   **65**

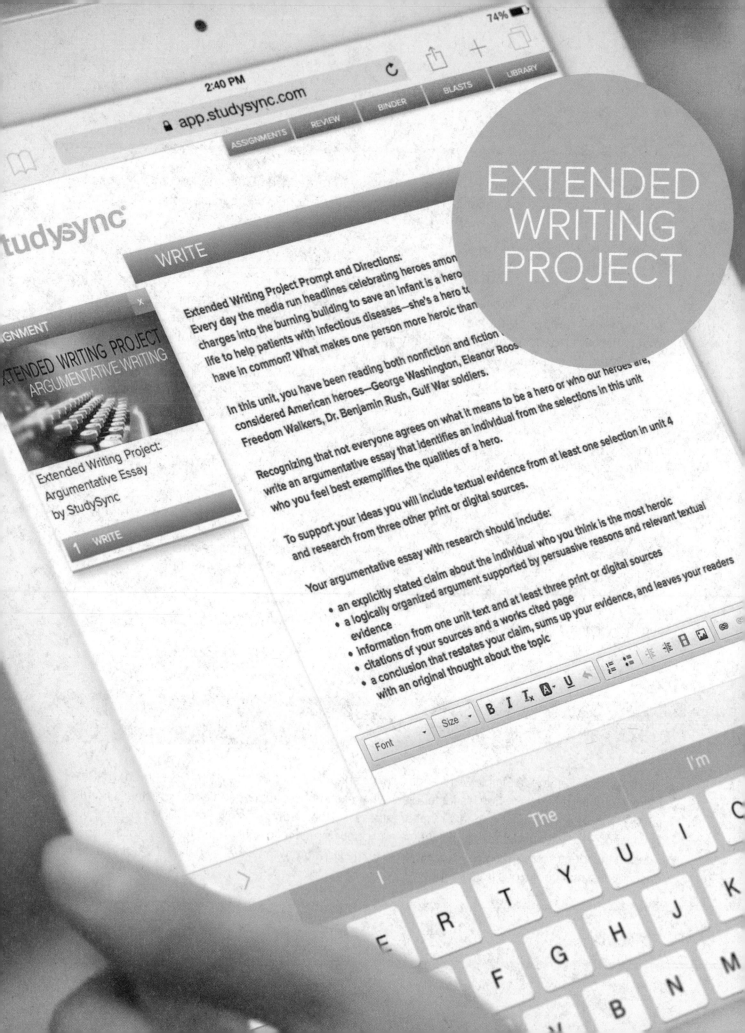

2:40 PM — 74%

app.studysync.com

ASSIGNMENTS | REVIEW | BINDER | BLASTS | LIBRARY

EXTENDED WRITING PROJECT

studysync

WRITE

Extended Writing Project Prompt and Directions:
Every day the media run headlines celebrating heroes amon[g]
charges into the burning building to save an infant is a hero [—]
life to help patients with infectious diseases—she's a hero t[o]
have in common? What makes one person more heroic than [...]

In this unit, you have been reading both nonfiction and fiction [...]
considered American heroes—George Washington, Eleanor Roos[evelt,]
Freedom Walkers, Dr. Benjamin Rush, Gulf War soldiers.

Recognizing that not everyone agrees on what it means to be a hero or who our heroes are,
write an argumentative essay that identifies an individual from the selections in this unit
who you feel best exemplifies the qualities of a hero.

To support your ideas you will include textual evidence from at least one selection in unit 4
and research from three other print or digital sources.

Your argumentative essay with research should include:

- an explicitly stated claim about the individual who you think is the most heroic
- a logically organized argument supported by persuasive reasons and relevant textual evidence
- information from one unit text and at least three print or digital sources
- citations of your sources and a works cited page
- a conclusion that restates your claim, sums up your evidence, and leaves your readers with an original thought about the topic

ASSIGNMENT

EXTENDED WRITING PROJECT
ARGUMENTATIVE WRITING

Extended Writing Project:
Argumentative Essay
by StudySync

1 WRITE

Font | Size | **B** *I* I x **A** U

The

I'm

ARGUMENTATIVE WRITING

WRITING PROMPT

Every day the media runs headlines celebrating heroes among us. The firefighter who charges into the burning building to save an infant is a hero. The nurse who risks her own life to help patients with infectious diseases—she's a hero too. What qualities do all heroes have in common? What makes one person more heroic than another?

In this unit, you have been reading both non-fiction and fiction texts about people who are considered American heroes—George Washington, Eleanor Roosevelt, Rosa Parks, the Freedom Walkers, Dr. Benjamin Rush, Gulf War soldiers.

Recognizing that not everyone agrees on what it means to be a hero or who our heroes are, write an argumentative essay that identifies an individual from the selections in this unit who you feel best exemplifies the qualities of a hero.

To support your ideas you will include textual evidence from at least one selection in unit 4 and research from three other print or digital sources.

Your argumentative essay with research should include:

- an explicitly stated claim about the individual who you think is the most heroic
- a logically organized argument supported by persuasive reasons and relevant textual evidence
- information from one unit text and at least three other print or digital sources

WRITING PROMPT

- citations of your sources and a Works Cited page
- a conclusion that restates your claim, sums up your reasons and evidence, and leaves your readers with an original thought about the topic

An **argumentative essay** is a form of persuasive writing. The writer's job is to make a claim about a topic, present logical reasons for making the claim, and then provide evidence—facts, details, and quotations—to support the claim. After first introducing the claim, the writer develops his or her ideas in the body of the argument, maintaining a formal style and using transitions to link related ideas. The purpose of the argument is for the writer to convince readers that his or her claim is valid. After presenting all the evidence to support his or her claim, the writer provides a concluding statement that follows from the argument presented.

In order to provide convincing supporting evidence, the writer must often do outside research, either because it is assigned or because it is essential to understanding a complex topic. That means the writer looks at print or digital sources of information related to the topic—books, articles, Web pages, diaries, letters, interviews, and other documents—and incorporates the information he or she finds into the argument. The writer cites these sources so that readers know where the supporting evidence was found and can confirm credibility. (In later Extended Writing Project Lessons, you will learn more about how to research a topic, including selecting appropriate material, effectively incorporating your research, and citing your sources.)

The features of an argumentative essay include:

- an introduction that states a claim, or an opinion, about the topic
- reasons and evidence that support the claim or claims
- a logical organizational structure with clear transitions
- embedded quotations from credible sources that are clearly cited
- a formal style that is maintained throughout the essay
- a concluding statement that follows from the argument presented

As you continue working on this Extended Writing Project, you'll learn more about crafting each of the elements of an argumentative essay with research.

STUDENT MODEL

Before you get started on your own argumentative essay, begin by reading one that a student wrote in response to the writing prompt. As you read this Student Model, highlight and annotate the features of an argumentative essay that the student included.

Rosa Parks: A True American Hero

Who is a hero? Many people might think that heroes have special powers and can save the world. But the superheroes we see in blockbuster movies and on TV are make-believe, and fighting monsters and stopping meteors are not real-life problems. As many of the selections in this unit show, true heroes live in the real world, take risks, and act as role models. For example, George Washington led a rebel army because he believed in an independent United States. Eleanor Roosevelt voiced the concerns of the poor during the Great Depression.

Both Washington and Roosevelt, who are considered heroes for good reasons, were also important leaders of their time. Washington was a general in the Continental Army and later president of the United States. Roosevelt was the First Lady of the United States. While they each had to confront huge obstacles, they were already respected citizens when they took up their causes. Rosa Parks, however, was an ordinary woman when she courageously refused to give up her bus seat and so changed American history. In defying authorities and the law, she committed an incredibly brave and even dangerous act. She did so with determination, grace, and dignity. The consequences of Parks's action—her arrest—and the African American community's response to it, helped launch the civil rights movement. This movement would make the United States a fairer place for everyone. Because, as an ordinary woman, she took great risks and acted peacefully and bravely on behalf of herself and others, I think she is the greatest hero we have read about in unit 4.

It's clear that Parks knew what she might face if she didn't obey the law. African Americans who defied the laws of segregation could face potential violence. As a child living in the South, she had seen her grandfather prepare to defend his family against the Ku Klux Klan ("Remembering Rosa Parks"). As an adult living in the segregated city of Montgomery, Alabama, in 1955, Parks understood the dangers of disobeying bus segregation policies. Civil rights leader Reverend

Joseph Lowery explained the possibilities in a 2005 interview: "The buses were particularly vicious in their policies . . . and it was especially humiliating to all the citizen[s] of Montgomery" ("Remembering Rosa Parks"). According to Parks's obituary in the *New York Times,* African Americans "had been arrested, even killed, for disobeying bus drivers" (Shipp). Indeed, her bravery surely was fed in part by anger and frustration that had built up over the years. As she wrote in her autobiography, she never considered obeying the bus driver: "I could not see how standing up was going to 'make it light' for me. The more we gave in and complied, the worse [whites] treated us" (Parks). Because of this history and her personal feelings, Parks decided to take action.

After her arrest, Parks continued to show great courage. She says she 'wasn't afraid," and yet she must have felt some fear (Parks). She knew that there was no guarantee she would get through the experience without physical harm. As a result, Parks really had a terrible choice to make: continuing to be treated as a second-class citizen or risking her freedom and perhaps even her life to reject segregation. She chose not to surrender to injustice.

What happened next was amazing, and it changed the course of American history. Parks's arrest did not go unnoticed. Congresswoman Eleanor Holmes Norton later called it "a quiet revolutionary act" that inspired a city and then a nation ("Remembering Rosa Parks"). Parks was "convicted of violating segregation laws and fined $4 in court fees" (Shipp). The law said Parks was in the wrong. However, more than 40,000 African Americans in Montgomery thought otherwise, and they took action. They did not react violently, but instead engaged in civil disobedience. In other words, they took lawful and peaceful steps toward making their voices heard. They struck back at the bus company by boycotting, or refusing to ride, the buses for 381 days (Shipp). The boycott was a great hardship for the people, but by not paying to ride buses, the African American community made its point.

During this time, lawyers contested bus segregation in court. The case went all the way to the Supreme Court, which finally banned segregation throughout the United States. So thanks to Rosa Parks, African Americans could ride a bus and sit wherever they chose without being harassed. According to Reverend Lowery, Parks's refusal to move her seat on a bus "triggered the greatest revolution in American history in terms of nonviolent protest against segregation and discrimination" ("Remembering Rosa Parks"). The movement she inspired caused many Americans to go on to fight peacefully, by way of marches and sit-ins, for African American voting rights and other social justice causes.

In standing up against a powerful segregated society, Rosa Parks reminded all Americans what equality means. In her autobiography, she summed up why she refused to move from her seat on the bus: "People always say that I didn't give up my seat because I was tired, but that isn't true . . . No, the only tired I was, was tired of giving in" (Parks). She channeled her anger peacefully. She took a huge risk and still maintained her dignity, serving as a model for others. I think in the end she made this country a better place to live for all people. Because of her efforts, among all the heroic men and women we have read about, she deserves to be honored as one of the greatest of American heroes.

Works Cited

Parks, Rosa, and James Haskins. *Rosa Parks: My Story*. New York: Dial Books, 1990. Print.

"Remembering Rosa Parks." PBS Newshour. 25 Oct. 2005. Web. 12 Dec. 2014. <http://www.pbs.org/newshour/bb/social_issues-july-dec05-parks_10-25>

Shipp, E.R. "Rosa Parks, 92, Founding Symbol of Civil Rights Movement, Dies." *New York Times*. 25 Oct. 2005. Web. 12 Dec. 2014. <http://www.nytimes.com/2005/10/25/us/25parks.html>

"Today in History: December 1." *The Library of Congress*. Web. 12 Dec. 2014 <http://memory.loc.gov/ammem/today/dec01.html>

Please note that excerpts and passages in the StudySync® library and this workbook are intended as touchstones to generate interest in an author's work. The excerpts and passages do not substitute for the reading of entire texts, and StudySync® strongly recommends that students seek out and purchase the whole literary or informational work in order to experience it as the author intended. Links to online resellers are available in our digital library. In addition, complete works may be ordered through an authorized reseller by filling out and returning to StudySync® the order form enclosed in this workbook.

Reading & Writing Companion

71

THINK QUESTIONS

1. The writer of the Student Model stated a claim about one of the individuals he or she read about in the unit. What is the writer's opinion about this person? What reason or reasons does the writer give? Where in the second paragraph of the Model did the writer state this claim and reasons?

2. What relevant textual evidence did the writer include in the Student Model to support his or her claim? Explain why the evidence is relevant.

3. Write two or three sentences evaluating the writer's conclusion in relation to the essay's claim, reasons, and evidence.

4. Thinking about the writing prompt, which selections or other resources would you like to use to write your own argumentative essay? What are some of the selections that you may want to consider as you think about which individual is the greatest hero?

5. Based on the selections you have read, listened to, or researched, how would you answer the question, *What does it mean to be a hero*? What are some ideas that you might consider in the argument you'll be developing?

PREWRITE

WRITING PROMPT

Every day the media runs headlines celebrating heroes among us. The firefighter who charges into the burning building to save an infant is a hero. The nurse who risks her own life to help patients with infectious diseases—she's a hero too. What qualities do all heroes have in common? What makes one person more heroic than another?

In this unit, you have been reading both non-fiction and fiction texts about people who are considered American heroes—George Washington, Eleanor Roosevelt, Rosa Parks, the Freedom Walkers, Dr. Benjamin Rush, Gulf War soldiers.

Recognizing that not everyone agrees on what it means to be a hero or who our heroes are, write an argumentative essay that identifies an individual from the selections in this unit who you feel best exemplifies the qualities of a hero.

To support your ideas you will include textual evidence from at least one selection in unit 4 and research from three other print or digital sources.

Your argumentative essay with research should include:

- an explicitly stated claim about the individual who you think is the most heroic
- a logically organized argument supported by persuasive reasons and relevant textual evidence
- information from one unit text and at least three other print or digital sources

WRITING PROMPT

- citations of your sources and a Works Cited page
- a conclusion that restates your claim, sums up your reasons and evidence, and leaves your readers with an original thought about the topic

Your first step—even before you start thinking about the person or group from the unit that you will write about—is to define what a hero is. Now is the time to start thinking about the qualities of a hero. You can use any of the prewriting strategies you have learned, including list making, brainstorming, freewriting, concept mapping, sketching, and so on. Begin by writing this sentence starter at the top of a blank sheet of paper: "I think a hero is someone who . . . ." Then fill the page with your ideas. You can jot words or phrases or draw pictures. After you have thought about what a hero is, write a complete sentence at the bottom of the page. Here's what the writer of the Student Model wrote: "I think a hero is someone who takes risks in order to make the world a better place to live."

Now flip over your sheet of paper. Use the back to answer these questions about the people you read about in the unit. As you answer the questions, think about your ideas about heroism. You can add your own questions to the list below, too.

- Which person from the unit was the bravest? What did he or she do that was brave? Did he or she feel brave at the time?
- Which person from the unit made the greatest sacrifice? What did he or she give up? Why?
- Which person from the unit did the most to make the world a better place to live? Give an example of that person's actions.
- Which person from the unit do I admire most? Why?

Look at the answers to your questions. Did you mention one person from the unit more than any other? Does that person exemplify your ideas about heroism? If so, you might have found the person who will be the topic of your argumentative essay.

Once you have identified your topic, the next step is to make a list of research questions. You want to ask questions that will lead you to evidence that supports your claim. The answers you uncover during your research will help you build an effective argument.

Use a graphic organizer like this one to help you get started with your own research. It shows some of the research questions that the writer of the Student Model asked about Rosa Parks. Notice how the student's questions try to get beyond the basic *who, what, where, when,* and *how questions*. The questions ask about how Parks felt, what she was thinking, and what kind of impact she had on the world. The questions show that the writer is trying to figure out why Parks was a heroic figure.

As you write your own questions in the left-hand column, think about the possible sources you might consult—history books, encyclopedia articles, news articles, memoirs, interviews, Web pages—for the answers. List the possible sources in the other column. (Later in the writing process, you can add a third column for the answers you find as you research your questions.)

Topic: Rosa Parks

Claim: Rosa Parks is a hero because she took serious risks to help make the world a fairer place for everyone.

RESEARCH QUESTIONS	POSSIBLE SOURCES
Why do most people consider Rosa Parks to be a hero?	history books, books and articles about the civil rights movement, Web pages
What risks did Rosa Parks face in refusing to give up her seat on a bus?	autobiography/memoir, interviews, civil rights memoirs and histories, newspaper articles
Why did Rosa Parks disobey the bus driver?	autobiography/memoir, interviews, history books
What impact did Rosa Parks's action have on history?	history books, encyclopedia articles, newspaper articles, news analyses
What are civil disobedience and the civil rights movement?	American history books, encyclopedia articles
What happened to Rosa Parks after she was arrested? After segregation was outlawed?	autobiography/memoir, interviews, history books
What was Rosa Parks really like as a person?	autobiography/memoir, interviews, history books

SKILL: RESEARCH AND NOTE-TAKING

⭐ DEFINE

If you have already completed the Research presentations for previous units or have been working on a Research presentation for this unit, you have already learned something about how to do research. **Research** is how you find new information or double-check facts or ideas that you don't know for sure. Research can be as straightforward as checking a word's meaning in the dictionary or as challenging as trying a new activity to get first-hand experience.

Unless you have a perfect memory (and few of us do), **note-taking** is essential to good research. Each time you check a source, you should take notes. A **source** might be a textbook, a newspaper article, a website, a dictionary, or an authority on a subject. Your **notes** should include the title of the source, its author's name, its date of publication, and any information and ideas you learned from it relevant to your research.

Why do you need all this in your notes? You might need to go back later to double-check a fact. You also need this information in order to prepare citations and a Works Cited section in your writing. Finally, your readers can use the information about your sources to do their own research.

Remember your purpose for doing research. In this unit, you are writing an argumentative essay. The point of your research is to find facts, details, and quotations that help support your claim about your topic.

••• IDENTIFICATION AND APPLICATION

- Your topic might be one that's assigned or one that you choose. Before you start your research, ask, *What don't I know about the topic?*
- Keep in mind questions you asked during prewriting as you think about your topic and do research. More questions should come up as you

research to help you determine what you really need to know and want to say.

- Enter specific keywords and phrases when researching online. You will likely have to experiment with the words and phrases in order to find accurate and reliable sources.

- Think about the accuracy and reliability of your sources. To choose sources carefully:

  › Look for reputable sources, such as fact-based newspapers, magazines, and academic journals.

  › Try to stick to educational and government websites (those ending in *.edu* and *.gov*).

- Remember the difference between primary sources (firsthand accounts) and secondary sources (secondhand accounts).

  › Autobiographies, journals, diaries, letters, interviews, and memoirs are primary sources.

  › Textbooks, encyclopedias articles, history books, and most newspaper articles are secondary sources.

- Stay focused when you take notes. To stay focused:

  › Look for the answers to your research questions.

  › Think about your purpose and audience.

  › Don't get distracted by irrelevant information.

- Take careful notes. If you prefer to write your notes on index cards, use one card for each source:

  › Be sure to include the title, author, and publication information on the card.

  › Number multiple cards for the same source in order.

- You can take notes digitally using note-taking apps, software, or a word processing program. To take digital notes using a word processing program, do the following:

  › Open a new document for each source.

  › At the top of the page, identify the title, author, and publication information.

  › Use bullets or new paragraphs for each new set of facts and information.

- If they are available, as in a book, include page numbers in your notes so you can remember where you found specific items of information.

- If you want to quote a source, write down the words exactly as they appear in the source and place them within quotation marks. Be sure to credit the source.

- Sometimes you might want to restate or paraphrase in your own words the ideas and words from a source. But you still must cite the original source so that readers know where you got the information.

- Cite your sources very carefully to avoid plagiarizing, or presenting other people's words and ideas as your own. Here's a rule of thumb: Anytime you use information from a researched source, give the writer credit.

 MODEL

Consider the following paragraph from the Student Model essay "Rosa Parks: A True American Hero":

> What happened next was amazing and **it changed the course of American history.** Parks's arrest did not go unnoticed. **Congresswoman Eleanor Holmes Norton later called it "a quiet revolutionary act"** that inspired a city and then a nation ("Remembering Rosa Parks"). Parks was **"convicted of violating segregation laws and fined $4 in court fees"** (Shipp). The law said Parks was in the wrong. However, more than 40,000 African Americans in Montgomery thought otherwise, and they took action. They did not react violently, but instead engaged in civil disobedience. In other words, they took lawful and peaceful steps toward making their voices heard. **Then they struck back at the bus company by boycotting, or refusing to ride, the buses for 381 days** (Shipp). The boycott was a great hardship for the people, but by not paying to ride buses, the African American community made its point.

Notice the research that the writer has included and the purpose it serves. After learning more about Parks from reading different sources, the writer decided to say that Parks's act helped "change the course of American history." To support this idea with evidence, the writer quotes a congresswoman, someone the writer discovered in the course of doing research. The congresswoman called what Parks did "a quiet revolutionary act," a comment that affirms the writer's own statement that history was changed. The writer tells readers the name of the congresswoman who made the remark and provides a parenthetical citation: ("Remembering Rosa Parks"). A quick glance at the Works Cited tells readers that the source is a reliable news program's website (*PBS Newshour,* at www.pbs.org). Later in the paragraph, the writer quotes from and also paraphrases information from Rosa Parks's obituary in the *New York Times,* written by E.R. Shipp. The writer has cited this source several times throughout the essay, so he or she does not need to introduce it every time.

Copyright © BookheadEd Learning, LLC

PRACTICE

Research a quotation about the person you will be discussing in your essay on heroism. Write down the quotation exactly as it appears in the source. Then for practice, restate the quotation in your own words and cite its source. As always, record the source's title, author, date, and publication information in your notes.

NOTES

SKILL: THESIS STATEMENT

DEFINE

The thesis of an argumentative essay takes the form of a claim. A claim is the writer's opinion about the topic of the essay. It is a statement of position, belief, or judgment. A claim might be introduced with certain phrases that make the writer's point of view clear, such as "I believe...," "I think...," "We should...," or "One must..." An opinion cannot be proven to be true, but it can be supported with relevant evidence—facts, statistics, quotations from experts, examples, and so on. The claim of an argument typically appears in the introductory section, often as the last sentence.

IDENTIFICATION AND APPLICATION

A thesis statement or claim in an argumentative essay:

- states an opinion about the topic of the essay
- previews the ideas and evidence that will be presented in the body paragraphs of the essay
- gets stated in the introductory section, which usually consists of one paragraph but may consist of two. You will learn more about crafting an introductory section in a later Extended Writing Project lesson.

MODEL

The following are the two introductory paragraphs from the Student Model argumentative essay, "Rosa Parks: A True American Hero":

> Who is a hero? Many people might think that heroes have special powers and can save the world. But the superheroes we see in blockbuster movies and on TV are make-believe, and fighting monsters and stopping meteors

are not real-life problems. As many of the selections in this unit show, true heroes live in the real world, take risks, and act as role models. For example, George Washington led a rebel army because he believed in an independent United States. Eleanor Roosevelt voiced the concerns of the poor during the Great Depression.

Both Washington and Roosevelt, who are considered heroes for good reasons, were also important leaders of their time. Washington was a general in the Continental Army and later president of the United States. Roosevelt was the First Lady of the United States. While they each had to confront huge obstacles, they were already respected citizens when they took up their causes. Rosa Parks, however, was an ordinary woman when she courageously refused to give up her bus seat and so changed American history. In defying authorities and the law, she committed an incredibly brave and even dangerous act. She did so with determination, grace, and dignity. The consequences of Parks's action—her arrest—and the African American community's response to it, helped launch the civil rights movement, which would make the United States a fairer place for everyone. **Because, as an ordinary woman, she took great risks and acted peacefully and bravely on behalf of herself and others, I think she is the greatest hero we have read about in unit 4.**

Notice the boldfaced claim at the end of the essay's second paragraph. This student's claim responds to the writing prompt by identifying the individual from the unit who the writer thinks best exemplifies the qualities of a hero. By using the words "I think," the writer makes clear that the thesis or claim expresses an opinion. Notice how the writer previews the ideas to be discussed in the body of the paper. He or she will present evidence to support the idea that Rosa Parks "took great risks and acted peacefully and bravely on behalf of herself and others."

 PRACTICE

Write a thesis statement in the form of a claim for your argumentative essay. Your statement should identify the individual you consider a hero and state a reason why you believe so. When you are finished writing your claim, exchange your work with a partner for peer review. How clear is your partner's claim? Is it obvious why he or she thinks the individual is a hero? How well does the claim address all the parts of the prompt? Offer suggestions and make constructive comments that will help your partner develop an effective thesis.

SKILL: ORGANIZE ARGUMENTATIVE WRITING

DEFINE

As you have learned, the purpose of argumentative writing is to persuade readers to accept the writer's thesis statement, or claim. To do so, the writer must organize and present his or her reasons and relevant evidence—the facts, examples, statistics, and quotations found during research —in a logical and convincing way. The writer must also select an **organizational structure** that best suits the argument.

The writer of argument can choose from a number of organizational structures, including **compare and contrast, order of importance, problem and solution, cause-effect, and chronological (or sequential) order.** Experienced writers use **transition words and phrases** in their writing to help readers understand which organizational structure is being used. As they plan, writers often use an outline or other graphic organizer to determine the best way to present their ideas and evidence most persuasively.

Writers are not limited to using only one organizational structure throughout a text. Within a specific section or paragraph, they might use one or more different organizational structures. This does not affect the overall organization, however.

IDENTIFICATION AND APPLICATION

- When selecting an overall organizational structure for an argument, a writer must consider the claim he or she is making. Then the writer needs to think about the best way to present the evidence that supports it. Do this by asking:

  › To support my claim, should I compare and contrast ideas or details in the text?

  › Is there an order of importance to my evidence? Is some evidence stronger than other evidence or does all my evidence support my claim equally well?

> › In my claim, have I raised a question or identified a problem? Do I have supporting evidence that suggests a solution or an answer?
> › Does my supporting evidence suggest a cause or an effect?
> › To support my claim, does it make sense to retell an events or series of events in chronological, or time, order?

• Writers often use specific transition words and phrases to help readers recognize the organizational structure of their writing:

> › Compare and contrast: *like, unlike, and, both, similar to, different from, while, but, in contrast, although, also*
> › Order of importance: *most, most important, least, least important, first, finally, mainly, to begin with*
> › Problem and solution: *problem, solution, why, how*
> › Cause-effect: *because, as a consequence of, as a result, cause, effect, so, in order to*

• Chronological order: *first, next, then, second, finally, before, after*

MODEL

During the prewriting stage, the writer of the Student Model figured out that Rosa Parks's actions had many causes and several important effects. The writer decided the best approach would be to use a cause-effect organizational structure for the argument.

At several points in the Student Model, the author uses transition words to show cause-effect relationships:

> **Because** of this history and her personal feelings, Parks decided to take action.

> **As a result,** Parks really had a terrible choice to make...

> **So** thanks to Rosa Parks, African Americans could ride a bus and sit wherever they chose without being harassed.

> **Because** of her efforts, among all the heroic men and women we have read about, she deserves to be honored as one of the greatest of American heroes.

Once a writer has selected the most appropriate organizational structure, he or she can use an outline or a graphic organizer (for example, a Venn diagram, flow chart, concept map, or timeline) to begin organizing the supporting evidence.

NOTES

The writer of the Student Model argument used the following graphic organizer during planning to organize the evidence that supports this claim:

Because, as an ordinary woman, she took great risks and acted peacefully and bravely on behalf of herself and others, I think she is the greatest hero we have read about in unit 4.

CAUSE	EFFECT
Parks took risks for others, was brave, acted peacefully	Parks is the greatest hero of all in the unit.
The South was segregated. The bus laws were vicious and humiliating. Parks was angry.	Parks refused to give up seat on bus.
Parks faced danger.	Parks had a tough choice to make.
Parks inspired the bus boycott.	Segregation was banned. A great peaceful revolution began.

 PRACTICE

Use an *Organize Argumentative Writing* graphic organizer like the one used with the Student Model, or choose one that better suits your organizational strategy. Fill in the organizer with evidence you gathered in the Prewrite stage of writing your argument.

Reading & Writing Companion

SKILL: SUPPORTING DETAILS

 ## DEFINE

The writer of an effective argument must provide **supporting details** in the form of reasons and relevant evidence. **Reasons** are statements that answer the question "Why?" They tell why the writer thinks his or her claim is true. A writer provides reasons to support a claim, which makes it more believable. **Relevant evidence** includes facts, statistics, definitions, quotations from experts, observations from eyewitnesses, and examples. Evidence that supports the reasons and the claim is often found through research.

Research can be the key to a successful argument. While researching, the writer deepens his or her understanding of the topic and finds evidence that supports the reasons and the claim. (Just as important—if the writer can't find enough evidence that supports the claim, then he or she knows it's time to change the claim or rethink the reasons.) Without solid supporting evidence, the writer would simply be stating his or her opinion about a topic—and that is rarely convincing to readers.

Because writers want to convince readers that their claims are credible, or believable, they carefully select and present the supporting details. A detail is **relevant** only if it supports the claim and helps build the argument. If the detail does not support the claim or strengthen the argument, it is irrelevant and should not be used.

 ## IDENTIFICATION AND APPLICATION

Step 1:

Review your claim. In your research, you want to find supporting details that are relevant to your claim. Ask the following question: "What am I trying to persuade my audience to believe?" That's what the writer of the Student Model did. Here's the claim:

Because as an ordinary woman [Parks] took great risks and acted peacefully and bravely on behalf of herself and others, I think she is the greatest hero we have read about in unit 4.

Step 2:

Ask what a reader needs to know about the topic in order to accept the claim. To understand a claim about the risks Parks took, for example, a reader must first know something about the world in which she lived. Why was it so dangerous for Rosa Parks to refuse to give up her seat on a bus? Here's the reason the writer gives:

> **African Americans who defied the laws of segregation could face potential violence.**

The writer provides several supporting details that back up that reason:

1. **As a child living in the South, she had seen her grandfather prepare to defend his family against the Ku Klux Klan ("Remembering Rosa Parks").**

2. **As an adult living in the segregated city of Montgomery, Alabama, in 1955, Parks understood the dangers of disobeying bus segregation policies.**

3. **Civil rights leader Reverend Joseph Lowery explained the possibilities in a 2005 interview: "The buses were particularly vicious in their policies . . . and it was especially humiliating to all the citizen[s] of Montgomery" ("Remembering Rosa Parks").**

4. **According to Parks's obituary in the *New York Times,* African Americans "had been arrested, even killed, for disobeying bus drivers" (Shipp).**

Most of these supporting details came from the writer's research. The details definitely support the writer's claim that Parks took risks.

Step 3:

You might find lots of details in your research, and you might want to use them all to support your claim, but it is important to evaluate each detail before you use it to make sure it is relevant and convincing. To do this, ask yourself the following questions:

- Does this information help the reader deepen his or her understanding of the topic?
- Does this information support my claim?
- Does this information help build my argument?
- Do I have stronger evidence that makes the same point?

If you can answer *yes* to the first three questions and *no* to the fourth, then definitely use the supporting detail in your argument.

 MODEL

The Student Model writer used evidence found during his or her research to support the part of the claim that says Parks acted peacefully and on behalf of others.

> What happened next was amazing, and it changed the course of American history. Parks's arrest did not go unnoticed. Congresswoman Eleanor Holmes Norton later called it "a quiet revolutionary act" that inspired a city and then a nation ("Remembering Rosa Parks"). Parks was "convicted of violating segregation laws and fined $4 in court fees" (Shipp). The law said Parks was in the wrong. However, more than 40,000 African Americans in Montgomery thought otherwise, and they took action. They did not react violently but instead engaged in civil disobedience. In other words, they took lawful and peaceful steps toward making their voices heard. They struck back at the bus company by boycotting, or refusing to ride, the buses for 381 days (Shipp). The boycott was a great hardship for the people, but by not paying to ride buses, the African American community made its point.

What supporting details does the writer use here? The writer provides a direct quotation from an expert, along with facts about the terms of Parks's conviction and fine. The writer also provides details about the African American community's peaceful but forceful boycott to support the claim about Parks taking peaceful action on behalf of others.

 PRACTICE

Write your claim. Below it, write some supporting details for your argumentative essay. Draw on the research you completed earlier in the Extended Writing Project. Then exchange your work with a partner. Use what you have learned about relevant supporting details to evaluate his or her work. Be constructive in your comments.

NOTES

EXTENDED WRITING PROJECT
PLAN

PLAN

WRITING PROMPT

Every day the media runs headlines celebrating heroes among us. The firefighter who charges into the burning building to save an infant is a hero. The nurse who risks her own life to help patients with infectious diseases—she's a hero too. What qualities do all heroes have in common? What makes one person more heroic than another?

In this unit, you have been reading both non-fiction and fiction texts about people who are considered American heroes—George Washington, Eleanor Roosevelt, Rosa Parks, the Freedom Walkers, Dr. Benjamin Rush, Gulf War soldiers.

Recognizing that not everyone agrees on what it means to be a hero or who our heroes are, write an argumentative essay that identifies an individual from the selections in this unit who you feel best exemplifies the qualities of a hero.

To support your ideas you will include textual evidence from at least one selection in unit 4 and research from three other print or digital sources.

Your argumentative essay with research should include:

- an explicitly stated claim about the individual who you think is the most heroic
- a logically organized argument supported by persuasive reasons and relevant textual evidence
- information from one unit text and at least three other print or digital sources

WRITING PROMPT

- citations of your sources and a Works Cited page
- a conclusion that restates your claim, sums up your reasons and evidence, and leaves your readers with an original thought about the topic

Review the organizational structure and information you used to complete your *Organize Argumentative Writing* graphic organizer. This organized information and your claim will help you create a road map to use for writing your argumentative essay.

Consider the following questions as you develop your main paragraph topics and their supporting details in the road map:

- Who is the subject of your essay?
- What claim (or argument) are you making about this subject? (How does this person best exemplify the qualities of a hero?)
- What are your reasons for making this claim?
- What specific reasons and relevant evidence from the unit selections and from your research can you use to support your claim?
- How can you best present the evidence so that it persuades your audience to accept your claim?

Use this model to get started with your road map:

Argumentative Essay Road Map

Claim: Rosa Parks is the greatest hero of all the people we have read about in unit 4 because she was an ordinary woman who took great risks and acted bravely on behalf of herself and others.

Paragraph 1 Topic: Rosa Parks bravely did not give up her seat even though she risked physical harm.

Supporting Detail #1: Parks remembered the danger her family faced from the Ku Klux Klan when she was a girl.

Supporting Detail #2: Quote from interview with Reverend Joseph Lowery about how Montgomery's bus segregation laws were "especially humiliating"

Supporting Detail #3: Quote from the obituary of Parks in the *New York Times* about how African Americans were treated when they disobeyed bus drivers

Supporting Detail #4: Despite the risks, Parks was angry and frustrated with segregation laws, so she resisted them. Quote from Parks about how whites treated African Americans.

Paragraph 2 Topic: Parks showed great courage even after being arrested.

Supporting Detail #1: Quote from Parks about how she "wasn't afraid," but she must have known she might face physical harm at the hands of the police

Supporting Detail #2: Parks preferred to face arrest and possible violence than be treated as a second-class citizen any longer.

Paragraph 3 Topic: Parks's courageous action spurred a nonviolent revolution to end segregation in the United States.

Supporting Detail #1: Quote from the *New York Times* about how after Parks's arrest, thousands of African Americans refused to ride the Montgomery city buses for 381 days

Supporting Detail #2: The Supreme Court ruled that bus segregation laws were unconstitutional throughout the country.

Supporting Detail #3: Quote from Reverend Lowery about how Parks's arrest and the bus boycott led to other acts of civil disobedience that helped fight segregation and other kinds of social injustice

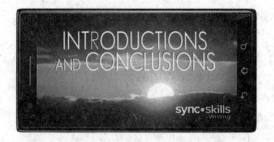

SKILL:
INTRODUCTIONS
AND
CONCLUSIONS

 DEFINE

The **introduction** is the opening paragraph or section of an argumentative essay or other non-fiction text. The introduction of an argumentative essay **identifies the topic to be discussed, states the writer's claim,** and **previews the supporting details** (reasons and evidence found during research) that will appear in the body of the text. The introduction is also the place where most writers include a **"hook"** that engages readers and helps them connect to the topic.

A **conclusion** is the closing paragraph or section of an argumentative essay or other type of non-fiction text. The conclusion is where the writer brings the argument to a close. The ideas presented in a conclusion follow directly from the introduction's claim and the supporting details provided in the body of the argument. In other words, it's where the writer restates the claim and sums up his or her evidence and research. In addition, the conclusion of an argument might also end with a call to action or an insightful comment.

 IDENTIFICATION AND APPLICATION

- In an argument, the introduction is the opening section in which the writer **identifies the topic to be discussed** and **directly states the claim.** The claim expresses the writer's opinion about the topic. By presenting the claim at the beginning of an argument, the writer lets readers know his or her position on the topic.

- The introduction is also where the writer provides a **preview of the reasons and evidence supporting the claim.** By doing so, the writer can establish an effective argument and increase the likelihood that readers will agree with the claim.

- An effective introduction has a "hook." A good hook engages readers' interest and makes them want to keep reading. A hook might be an intriguing image, a surprising detail, an interesting question, a funny anecdote, or a shocking statistic. The hook should also help readers connect to the topic in a meaningful way.

- An effective conclusion **restates the writer's claim** and **briefly summarizes the most convincing and strongest reasons and researched evidence** from the body paragraphs.

- Some conclusions offer some form of **insight** relating to the argument. The insightful comment is the last chance the writer has to persuade and even inspire readers to think or believe something. The insight may take any of the following forms:

  › An answer to a question first posed in the introduction
  › A question designed to elicit reflection on the part of the reader
  › A memorable or inspiring message
  › A last compelling example
  › A suggestion that readers learn more

 ## MODEL

The introduction and conclusion of the Student Model, "Rosa Parks: A True American Hero," contain many of the key elements discussed above. Consider the introduction:

> **Who is a hero? Many people might think that heroes have special powers and can save the world. But the superheroes we see in blockbuster movies and on TV are make-believe, and fighting monsters and stopping meteors are not real-life problems.** As many of the selections in this unit show, true heroes live in the real world, take risks, and act as role models. For example, George Washington led a rebel army because he believed in an independent United States. Eleanor Roosevelt voiced the concerns of the poor during the Great Depression.

> Both Washington and Roosevelt, who for good reasons are considered heroes, were also important leaders of their time. Washington was a general in the Continental Army and later president of the United States. Roosevelt was the First Lady of the United States. While they each had to confront huge obstacles, they were already respected citizens when they took up their causes. **Rosa Parks, however, was an ordinary woman when she courageously refused to give up her bus seat and so changed American history.** In defying authorities and the law, **she committed an incredibly brave and even dangerous act.** She did so with determination, grace, and

dignity. Moreover, she accepted the consequences of her action—arrest—and went through legal channels to protest and change the law. In addition, **her so-called "crime" and her arrest helped launch the civil rights movement.** This movement would make the United States a fairer place for everyone. **Because, as an ordinary woman, she took great risks and acted peacefully and bravely on behalf of herself and others, I think she is the greatest hero we have read about in unit 4.**

The introductory section of the Student Model consists of two paragraphs. Paragraph 1 of the introduction **"hooks"** readers by asking a question and by referring to "heroes" with "special powers," "superheroes," and "summer blockbuster movies." Then, in paragraph 2, the writer identifies the **topic**—Rosa Parks. The details about Parks not only hint at the evidence that will follow in the body of the argument, they also lead directly to the writer's **claim**—that Parks "is the greatest hero we have read about in unit 4." The sentence that includes the claim also previews some of the reasons the writer will discuss in the body of the essay.

Now consider the concluding paragraph of the Student Model:

In standing up against a powerful segregated society, Rosa Parks reminded Americans what equality means. In her autobiography, she summed up why she refused to move from her seat on the bus: "People always say that I didn't give up my seat because I was tired, but that isn't true . . . No, the only tired I was, was tired of giving in" (Parks). **She channeled her anger peacefully. She took a huge risk and still maintained her dignity, serving as a model for others. I think in the end she made this country a better place to live for all people. Because of her efforts, among all the heroic men and women we have read about, she deserves to be honored as one of the greatest of American heroes.**

The concluding paragraph **restates the claim, sums up the most important reasons,** and includes this **insightful comment:** "In standing up against a powerful segregated society, Parks reminded all Americans about what equality means."

 PRACTICE

Write an introduction and a conclusion for your argument. Your introduction should include a "hook," identify your topic, state your claim, and hint at the

NOTES

supporting details (reasons and evidence from your research) that will appear in the body of the essay. Then draft a conclusion that mirrors your introduction by restating your claim and summing up your research. Try to include an insightful comment about your topic or your claim. Finally, trade your work with a peer for review. Provide helpful feedback on your peer's introductions and conclusion.

SKILL: BODY
PARAGRAPHS
AND
TRANSITIONS

NOTES

 DEFINE

Body paragraphs appear between the introduction and conclusion of an argumentative essay. Together, they form the section in which a writer supports his or her claim with reasons and evidence collected during research. In general, each body paragraph should focus on one idea or reason so that the reader can easily follow along. The ideas in each body paragraph should support the claim.

It's important to structure a body paragraph clearly. Here is one way to structure the body paragraph of an argumentative essay:

- **Topic sentence:** The topic sentence is the first sentence of a body paragraph. It states the main point of the paragraph. The topic sentence should relate to your claim.

- **Evidence #1:** You should provide evidence that supports your topic sentence. Evidence can include relevant facts, definitions, observations, quotations, and examples.

- **Evidence #2:** Continue to develop your claim with a second piece of evidence.

- **Analysis/Explanation:** After presenting evidence, you should explain how the evidence helps support your topic sentence—and general claim—about the topic. Analysis is important in an argumentative essay. It is how you make sure that readers understand the connections you are making between the supporting evidence and the claim.

- **Concluding sentence:** After presenting your evidence and analysis, wrap up the main idea in a concluding sentence.

As you write body paragraphs, think carefully about how to incorporate your evidence. **Quotations** are an excellent form of evidence, but they need to be integrated into your writing carefully, or they will sound awkward. Always place the exact words of the quotations within quotation marks. Then end the sentence with a citation, so readers know where the quoted material comes from.

Please note that excerpts and passages in the StudySync® library and this workbook are intended as touchstones to generate interest in an author's work. The excerpts and passages do not substitute for the reading of entire texts, and StudySync® strongly recommends that students seek out and purchase the whole literary or informational work in order to experience it as the author intended. Links to online resellers are available in our digital library. In addition, complete works may be ordered through an authorized reseller by filling out and returning to StudySync® the order form enclosed in this workbook.

Reading & Writing
Companion

95

Compare these examples of a poorly integrated and well-integrated quotation:

Poorly integrated quotation:

> Parks's arrest did not go unnoticed. It was "a quiet revolutionary act." That was what Congresswoman Eleanor Holmes Norton said about Parks's arrest at a later time.

Well integrated quotation:

> Congresswoman Eleanor Holmes Norton later called it "a quiet revolutionary act" that inspired a city and then a nation ("Remembering Rosa Parks").

Remember, if a full quotation is too long, you can use **ellipses** (...) to show the parts that you left out—like this:

> "People always say that I didn't give up my seat because I was tired, but that isn't true... No, the only tired I was, was tired of giving in" (Parks).

You can also **paraphrase** the quotation—or any of your evidence. Paraphrasing involves restating information in your own words. For example, the writer of the Student Model used specific facts and figures from one of Parks's obituaries but used his or her own words to present the information and also cited the source:

> **The law said Parks was in the wrong, but more than 40,000 African Americans in Montgomery thought otherwise,** and they took action. However, they did not react violently, but rather engaged in civil disobedience. In other words, they took lawful and peaceful steps toward making their voices heard. Then **they struck back at the bus company by boycotting, or refusing to ride, the buses for 381 days (Shipp).**

Transitions are connecting words and phrases that writers use to clarify the relationships between ideas in a text. Transitions help make connections between words in a sentence and ideas in individual paragraphs. They also help indicate the organizational structure of a text. Adding transition words or phrases to the beginning or end of a paragraph can help a writer guide readers smoothly through a text.

IDENTIFICATION AND APPLICATION

- Body paragraphs are the section of the argumentative essay between the introduction and conclusion. These paragraphs provide reasons and supporting evidence. Typically, writers of arguments focus on one main idea in each body paragraph.

  › A topic sentence clearly states the main idea of that paragraph. The main idea should support and relate to the writer's main claim. The main idea may provide one of the reasons for making the claim.

  › Evidence consists of relevant facts, definitions, observations, quotations, and examples.

  › Analysis and explanation tell how the evidence supports the topic sentence and the claim.

  › A conclusion sentence wraps up the paragraph's main idea.

- Certain transition words and phrases indicate specific organizational relationships within a text. Here are some examples:

  › Cause-effect: *because, accordingly, as a result, so, for, since, therefore, if, then*

  › Compare and contrast: *like, unlike, also, both, similarly, although, while, but, however, whereas, meanwhile, on the contrary, yet, still*

  › Chronological order: *first, then, next, finally, before, after, when, following, within a few years*

- Transition words and phrases also help readers connect ideas and information in a text, as well as understand the relationship among the claim, reasons, and evidence. A phrase like *for example* can help show the relationship between a main point and its evidence. The phrase *in addition* to can help link similar ideas.

- Quotations are an excellent form of evidence. You can include direct quotes from sources in your writing or paraphrase a quote in your own words. To avoid **plagiarism,** be sure to introduce the source of the quotation before you quote it.

  › When using a direct quote, always place the exact words of the quotations within quotation marks.

  › Whenever you paraphrase or provide a direct quote, always end the sentence with a citation, so readers know where the paraphrased or quoted material comes from.

Please note that excerpts and passages in the StudySync® library and this workbook are intended as touchstones to generate interest in an author's work. The excerpts and passages do not substitute for the reading of entire texts, and StudySync® strongly recommends that students seek out and purchase the whole literary or informational work in order to experience it as the author intended. Links to online resellers are available in our digital library. In addition, complete works may be ordered through an authorized reseller by filling out and returning to StudySync® the order form enclosed in this workbook.

Reading & Writing Companion **97**

MODEL

The Student Model uses a body paragraph structure to develop the claim. It also includes transitions to help the reader understand the relationship between ideas and to indicate the text's organizational structure.

Read the second body paragraph from the Student Model, "Rosa Parks: A True American Hero." Look closely at the structure and think about how the writer incorporated his or her research. Look at the transition words and phrases in bold. How effective is the paragraph's structure? Does it develop ideas related to the claim? How do the transition words and phrases help you understand the text's organizational structure and the relationships between and among ideas?

> **After** her arrest, Parks continued to show great courage. **She says she "wasn't afraid,"** and yet she must have felt some fear (Parks). She knew that there was no guarantee she would get through the experience without physical harm. **As a result,** Parks really had a terrible choice to make: continuing to be treated as a second-class citizen or risking her freedom and perhaps even her life to reject segregation. **She chose not to surrender to injustice.**

The **topic sentence** of this paragraph presents one reason the writer has claimed that Rosa Parks is a great hero. Even after her arrest, she showed courage. The topic sentence is immediately followed by **evidence** in the form of a **quotation.** The writer neatly **integrates** the quotation. He or she makes clear whose words are used and follows them with his or her own ideas. The word *after* acts as a **transition** from the previous paragraph; it lets readers know they are reading about events in a sequence. The phrase *as a result* indicates a cause-effect relationship between Parks's fear and her action. The paragraph wraps up with the writer's **analysis.** The **concluding sentence** sums up what happened.

PRACTICE

Write one of the body paragraphs of your essay following the format above. When you finish writing, take a few minutes to think about what you've written. Then go back and edit your paragraph. Make sure you used clear transitions and check that you have chosen strong facts, details, and quotations to support your topic sentence. Ask yourself whether you have integrated your research smoothly and correctly. When you are finished, exchange your work with a partner. Offer each other constructive feedback by answering the following questions:

- How well does the topic sentence introduce the topic of the paragraph?

- How effectively does the topic sentence refer back to the claim?

- How strong is the evidence and analysis used to support the topic sentence?

- How well did the writer integrate quotes and paraphrased evidence? Did the writer cite this evidence properly?

- How do transitions help guide readers through the text? What functions do they serve?

- How well did the writer sum up ideas in the concluding sentence?

DRAFT

WRITING PROMPT

Every day the media runs headlines celebrating heroes among us. The firefighter who charges into the burning building to save an infant is a hero. The nurse who risks her own life to help patients with infectious diseases—she's a hero too. What qualities do all heroes have in common? What makes one person more heroic than another?

In this unit, you have been reading both non-fiction and fiction texts about people who are considered American heroes—George Washington, Eleanor Roosevelt, Rosa Parks, the Freedom Walkers, Dr. Benjamin Rush, Gulf War soldiers.

Recognizing that not everyone agrees on what it means to be a hero or who our heroes are, write an argumentative essay that identifies an individual from the selections in this unit who you feel best exemplifies the qualities of a hero.

To support your ideas you will include textual evidence from at least one selection in unit 4 and research from three other print or digital sources.

Your argumentative essay with research should include:

- an explicitly stated claim about the individual who you think is the most heroic

- a logically organized argument supported by persuasive reasons and relevant textual evidence

- information from one unit text and at least three other print or digital sources

WRITING PROMPT

- citations of your sources and a Works Cited page
- a conclusion that restates your claim, sums up your reasons and evidence, and leaves your readers with an original thought about the topic

You've already begun working on your own argumentative essay. So far, you've thought about your purpose, audience, and topic. You've carefully examined the unit texts and selected the individual you consider to be the greatest hero. You have also completed some outside research to gather information and evidence that supports your claim. If the evidence you found did not support your claim, you have refocused your ideas and claim as necessary. You've decided how to organize information, and you've gathered supporting details in the form of reasons and relevant evidence. You've carefully evaluated the argument you plan to make in order to ensure that you can support it fully with facts, details, and quotations. Now it's time to write a draft of your argument.

Use your road map and your other prewriting materials to help you as you write. Remember that an argument begins with an introduction that features a claim. Body paragraphs then develop the claim by providing clear reasons and relevant supporting details such as facts, details, quotations, and examples. Body paragraphs also provide your analysis of the evidence. Transitions signal an organizational structure and help the reader understand how the claim, reasons, and evidence are connected. A concluding paragraph restates or reinforces the claim and important points from the argument you have made. The conclusion may also share an original thought with your readers.

When drafting, ask yourself these questions:

- How can I make my hook more effective?
- What can I do to clarify my claim?
- Which relevant evidence from the unit text (or texts) and outside sources—including facts, direct quotations, examples, and observations—best supports my claim?
- How can I improve the structure of my argument by using better transitions?
- How convincing is my analysis of the evidence in support of my claim?

- How can I effectively restate my claim in the conclusion?
- What final message do I want to leave with my readers?

Be sure to carefully read your draft before you submit it. You want to make sure you've addressed every part of the prompt.

SKILL: SOURCES AND CITATIONS

 DEFINE

Sources are the texts that writers use to research their writing. A **primary source** is a first-hand account of events by the person who experienced them. Another type of source is known as a **secondary source.** This is a source that analyzes or interprets primary sources. **Citations** are notes that provide information about the source texts. It is necessary for a writer to provide a citation if he or she quotes a source directly, refers to ideas from a source, or includes specific facts and figures from a source. The citation lets readers know where the information originally came from.

 IDENTIFICATION AND APPLICATION

- Sources can be either primary or secondary. Primary sources are first-hand accounts or original materials such as the following:
  › Letters or other correspondence
  › Photographs
  › Official documents
  › Diaries or journals
  › Autobiographies or memoirs
  › Eyewitness accounts and interviews
  › Audio recordings and radio broadcasts
  › Literary texts, such as novels, poems, fables, and dramas
  › Works of art
  › Artifacts

- Secondary sources are usually texts. These texts are the written interpretation and analysis of primary source materials. Some examples of secondary sources include:
  › Encyclopedia articles
  › Textbooks
  › Commentary or criticisms

> Histories
> Documentary films
> News analyses

- Whether sources are primary or secondary, they must be **credible** and **reliable.**

- When a writer quotes directly from a source, he or she must copy the words exactly as they appear in the source, placing them within quotation marks. The writer must also cite the source of the quotation. Here's an example from the Student Model:

> Civil rights leader Reverend Joseph Lowery explained the possibilities in a 2005 interview, **"The buses were particularly vicious in their policies . . . and it was especially humiliating to all the citizen[s] of Montgomery"** ("Remembering Rosa Parks").

- One way to cite the source of a quotation is to put the information in parentheses at the end of the sentence. Another way is to mention the source in the context of the sentence. Sometimes the speaker of a quotation is different from the source where it was found. In that case, the speaker usually is mentioned in the sentence itself and the source in parentheses, as in the example of Reverend Lowry's quotation above.

- Information in parentheses includes either the last name of the source's author or the source's title, if an author is not named. If a page number is available, for example from a book, also cite the page number.

- Writers must also provide citations when borrowing ideas or specific facts and figures from another source, even when writers are paraphrasing, or putting the information into their own words. Citations serve both to credit the source and help readers find out where they can learn more.

- There are several styles of citation in addition to the parenthetical style. Ask your teacher to identify the style he or she prefers.

  > Writers who cite from sources in the body of their writing need to provide a **Works Cited** section that lists all the sources the writer used. As with citations, there are different styles of Works Cited lists, but the sources are always listed in alphabetical order by author's name. If the source has no author, then it is alphabetized by title.

 MODEL

Writers do research in order to answer questions they may have about a topic or to learn about a topic in greater depth or detail than what they already know. When they conduct research, writers should draw on credible and reliable sources, both to check the accuracy of information and add to their knowledge. They should always cite their sources. In this excerpt from the Student Model, "Rosa Parks: A True American Hero," the writer quotes from two different sources and identifies each quotations' source.

> What happened next was amazing, and it changed the course of American history. Parks's arrest did not go unnoticed. **Congresswoman Eleanor Holmes Norton later called it "a quiet revolutionary act"** that inspired a city and then a nation **("Remembering Rosa Parks")**. Parks was **"convicted of violating segregation laws and fined $4 in court fees" (Shipp)**. The law said Parks was in the wrong. However, more than 40,000 African Americans in Montgomery thought otherwise, and they took action. They did not react violently, but instead engaged in civil disobedience. In other words, they took lawful and peaceful steps toward making their voices heard. **They struck back at the bus company by boycotting, or refusing to ride, the buses for 381 days (Shipp)**. The boycott was a great hardship for the people, but by not paying to ride buses, the African American community made its point.

Notice that only the portions of text taken directly from the source appear in quotations and that the author's last name or the title of the source appears in parentheses after each quotation. Also notice that the author's last name appears in parentheses after the paraphrased ideas in sentence 9.

Here is how the writer's sources appear in the Works Cited section that follows the argumentative essay:

Works Cited

Parks, Rosa, and James Haskins. *Rosa Parks: My Story*. New York: Dial Books, 1990. Print.

"Remembering Rosa Parks." *PBS Newshour*. 25 Oct. 2005. Web. **12 Dec. 2014.**
<**http://www.pbs.org/newshour/bb/social_issues-july-dec05-parks_10-25**>

Shipp, E.R. "Rosa Parks, 92, Founding Symbol of Civil Rights Movement, Dies." *New York Times*. 25 Oct. 2005. Web. **12 Dec. 2014.**
<http://www.nytimes.com/2005/10/25/us/25parks.html>

"**Today** in History: December 1." *The Library of Congress.* Web. **12 Dec. 2014.**

<http://memory.loc.gov/ammem/today/dec01.html>

Notice how the sources are listed alphabetically by the author's last name (or by the title if the source has no author). The author's name is followed by the title and the publication information. When a source is published online, the writer needs to identify its URL and give the date of when he or she accessed it. From this Works Cited section, you can tell that the writer accessed all three online sources on the same day.

 PRACTICE

If you have not yet written your Works Cited section, do so now. Go back to your draft and check that you have cited your sources correctly. Edit your citations, making sure they follow the conventions your teacher recommended. Then exchange your Works Cited section with a partner and provide each other with feedback. Look carefully at how your partner formatted and punctuated the citations. Edit and provide constructive feedback.

NOTES

REVISE

Copyright © BookheadEd Learning, LLC

WRITING PROMPT

Every day the media runs headlines celebrating heroes among us. The firefighter who charges into the burning building to save an infant is a hero. The nurse who risks her own life to help patients with infectious diseases—she's a hero too. What qualities do all heroes have in common? What makes one person more heroic than another?

In this unit, you have been reading both non-fiction and fiction texts about people who are considered American heroes—George Washington, Eleanor Roosevelt, Rosa Parks, the Freedom Walkers, Dr. Benjamin Rush, Gulf War soldiers.

Recognizing that not everyone agrees on what it means to be a hero or who our heroes are, write an argumentative essay that identifies an individual from the selections in this unit who you feel best exemplifies the qualities of a hero.

To support your ideas you will include textual evidence from at least one selection in unit 4 and research from three other print or digital sources.

Your argumentative essay with research should include:

- an explicitly stated claim about the individual who you think is the most heroic
- a logically organized argument supported by persuasive reasons and relevant textual evidence
- information from one unit text and at least three other print or digital sources

WRITING PROMPT

- citations of your sources and a Works Cited page
- a conclusion that restates your claim, sums up your reasons and evidence, and leaves your readers with an original thought about the topic

You have written a draft of your argumentative essay. You have also received input from your peers about how to improve it. Now you are going to revise your draft.

Here are some recommendations to help you revise:

- Review the suggestions made by your peers. You don't have to implement every suggestion, but think seriously about your peers' comments as you revise.

- Focus on maintaining a formal style and tone. A formal style suits your purpose—persuading readers to agree with your ideas about a topic. It is also appropriate for your audience—students, teachers, and other readers interested in learning more about your topic. Your tone, or attitude toward your topic, should be serious, thoughtful, and respectful. It should help indicate that you fully understand your topic.

  › Use standard English in your writing. As you revise, eliminate any informal language, particularly slang, unless it is included in quoted material or is essential to readers' understanding.
  › Review your language. Look for words and phrases that are too general or overused. Think of more precise words or specialized vocabulary to replace them. Provide definitions, if you think your readers will need them.
  › Pay attention to pronouns. Make sure you have used the proper pronoun (same number and case) to replace the noun it refers to in a sentence. Check that you have punctuated all possessive pronouns properly.
  › Incorporate a variety of sentence structures into your writing. Check that you aren't beginning every sentence the same way. A mixture of sentence lengths and types will create an interesting pattern that will keep readers engaged in your writing.

- After you have revised for elements of style and tone, use these questions to review your argument for ways you could improve its organization and supporting details:

› Is your organizational structure apparent? Would your argument flow better if you added more transitions between sentences and paragraphs? What transition words best suit your organizational structure?

› What additional evidence, such as quotations and facts, might you want to add in order to fully support your claim and reasons for making the claim?

› How well have you incorporated quotations into your sentences and paragraphs? Are the quotations clearly introduced and punctuated properly? Have you double-checked your citations to make sure you have correctly cited the source of the quotation in the body of the paper and in the Works Cited section?

EDIT,
PROOFREAD,
AND PUBLISH

WRITING PROMPT

Every day the media runs headlines celebrating heroes among us. The firefighter who charges into the burning building to save an infant is a hero. The nurse who risks her own life to help patients with infectious diseases—she's a hero too. What qualities do all heroes have in common? What makes one person more heroic than another?

In this unit, you have been reading both non-fiction and fiction texts about people who are considered American heroes—George Washington, Eleanor Roosevelt, Rosa Parks, the Freedom Walkers, Dr. Benjamin Rush, Gulf War soldiers.

Recognizing that not everyone agrees on what it means to be a hero or who our heroes are, write an argumentative essay that identifies an individual from the selections in this unit who you feel best exemplifies the qualities of a hero.

To support your ideas you will include textual evidence from at least one selection in unit 4 and research from three other print or digital sources.

Your argumentative essay with research should include:

- an explicitly stated claim about the individual who you think is the most heroic
- a logically organized argument supported by persuasive reasons and relevant textual evidence
- information from one unit text and at least three other print or digital sources

WRITING PROMPT

- citations of your sources and a Works Cited page
- a conclusion that restates your claim, sums up your reasons and evidence, and leaves your readers with an original thought about the topic

Now that you have revised your argumentative essay and received feedback from your peers, it's time to edit and proofread to produce a final version. Have you taken into consideration all the suggestions from your peers? Ask yourself these questions:

- Have I presented a persuasive argument?
- Have I fully supported my claim with strong reasons and relevant textual evidence?
- Is the organization of information clear and easy for the reader to follow?
- Have I correctly cited my sources?
- Would my argument benefit from additional transitions?
- Have I used a variety of effective sentence structures? Have I used a formal style and tone throughout?
- What else can I do to improve my essay's information and organization?

Once you are satisfied with your work, proofread it for grammatical and mechanical errors. For example:

- Are all your pronouns in the proper case?
- Have you used the correct punctuation for quotations and citations?
- Have you capitalized all proper nouns?

Be sure to correct any misspelled words you find in your argument. If you're uncertain about the spelling of a word, double-check your work by looking in a dictionary.

Once you have made all your corrections, you are ready to submit and publish your work. You can distribute your writing to family and friends, or post it at school or online. If you do decide to publish online, include links to your sources and citations. This will enable readers to learn more from the sources on their own time. You might also take an opportunity to deliver your argumentative essay as an oral presentation to friends, family, or classmates. They might welcome the chance to hear your ideas about someone you consider to be a hero.

Text Fulfillment
Through StudySync

If you are interested in specific titles, please fill out the form below and we will check availability through our partners.

ORDER DETAILS

Date:

TITLE	AUTHOR	Paperback/Hardcover	Specific Edition *If Applicable*	Quantity

SHIPPING INFORMATION

Contact:

Title:

School/District:

Address Line 1:

Address Line 2:

Zip or Postal Code:

Phone:

Mobile:

Email:

BILLING INFORMATION ☐ *SAME AS SHIPPING*

Contact:

Title:

School/District:

Address Line 1:

Address Line 2:

Zip or Postal Code:

Phone:

Mobile:

Email:

PAYMENT INFORMATION

☐ CREDIT CARD

Name on Card:

Card Number: Expiration Date: Security Code:

☐ PO

Purchase Order Number:

StudySync Text Fulfillment, BookheadEd Learning, LLC
610 Daniel Young Drive | Sonoma, CA 95476